Doorway
to
Your
Destiny

Jo Naughton

**Grosvenor House
Publishing Limited**

The right of Healed for Life to be identified as the author of this
work has been asserted in accordance with Section 78
of the Copyright, Designs and Patents Act 1988

The book cover picture is copyright to Healed for Life

This book is published by
Grosvenor House Publishing Ltd
Link House
140 The Broadway, Tolworth, Surrey, KT6 7HT.
www.grosvenorhousepublishing.co.uk

A CIP record for this book
is available from the British Library

ISBN 978-1-78623-074-4

Names and details have been changed to protect the identity
of the people mentioned. Bible references are from
the New King James version unless otherwise stated.
The Message is also used to help reveal
the heart of certain passages.

Contents

This book is dedicated to my dad.
I have learned more from you than you could ever know.

THANK YOU

Thank you Paolo for being
God's number one tool of transformation in my life.

Thank you Larissa for standing
by me and strengthening me through every up and down.

Thank you Prophet Cathy for being
my mentor, my second mama and my friend.

Thank you Tim for investing
your time and talents into our lives and ministry.

Chapter 1

YOUR STORY

It's a long story (for most of us...)

God loves to plant His promises in our hearts. As we draw near to Him, He gives us desires and dreams for a fulfilling life. He begins to paint a picture of destiny within our souls. Soon, we're hungry for realization. Then the wait begins. Occasionally, we see it all come to pass promptly. All too often, it feels like an eternity. If that wasn't enough, this period may be marred by pain and pressure. Although the longing for a better future burns within, circumstances look hopeless and disappointment creeps in. It is in this place that we usually come face to face with one of God's choice tools for maturing His people. It is called *process* and it is God's mechanism for making us into men and women that are ready for our destiny.

On your marks, get set...

I got saved when I was 12 and was filled with the Holy Spirit when I was 15 years old. I loved the Lord with all of my heart and was full of zeal. I shared the gospel with anyone who would listen and was daily in the Word and prayer. But I had lots of issues. When I left home, I backslid into a life of partying. For about three years, I went to the wrong places with the wrong people and did wrong things. If you are praying for a prodigal, please don't give up. I believe that the prayers of people who loved me brought me through and I rededicated my life to the Lord in my early twenties. I enrolled in Bible college, started working for the church and embarked on a new life dedicated to Christ. I had a strong sense of the call of God and believed I was ready to go to the nations with the glory of God. I could not have been more wrong.

My family suffered a great deal while I was growing up, but that was the only life I knew so I thought I was fine. As an adult, the cracks in my self-worth showed, although I didn't know it at the time. I craved recognition and reassurance. Job titles, ministry position, achievements and even having a family gave me a sense of validity. It was after a decade of marriage and ministry that God started a life-altering work within me. He shined His light into the depths of my heart and revealed the truth. The reality was that if you were to strip away my titles and talents, I did not feel good enough. I broke and God took me on an incredible journey to genuine security. He restored me in areas where I did not even realize I was broken. God healed, honed and humbled. He restored, re-wired and refined. Of course, I am still a work in progress but I'm so thankful for my process.

Saul's sad story

Some of the saddest stories in Scripture are about people who missed the mark. I don't mean the likes of King David who messed up but repented. I am referring to the Samsons and Sauls of the Old Testament. People who God chose but who lacked the character to carry the anointing on their lives. If success had not come so easily to them, I sometimes wonder whether they would have developed the character to fulfil their call. Either way, I thank the Lord that their lives are described in detail for our benefit. The Bible tells their stories so that we can learn from their mistakes.

I believe King Saul is often misunderstood. We see him as the enemy that David had to overthrow. But when Israel asked for a king, the Lord selected Saul. He was God's choice to lead His precious people. The Lord picked him because he was a good man with a good heart. 1 Samuel 9:2 in Young's Literal Translation describes Saul like this: "There is not a man among the sons of Israel goodlier than he." Sadly, success amplified the faults in his foundations. Saul had deep feelings of inadequacy. Right from the start, he doubted his ability to be king. He even hid when he was due to be presented to the nation as their new leader.

It is the same for you and me. If we secretly struggle with insecurities when we are small in the world's eyes, our issues will only be magnified when we reach the limelight. If we hanker after affirmation when we are a 'nobody', we will feed on public approval when we become a 'somebody'. It can be a deadly trap.

We don't know why Saul battled with low self-esteem. Perhaps he felt like a failure growing up under the shadow of a wealthy father who forgot to affirm him. The Bible very clearly states that his dad, Kish, was a powerful and wealthy man. It can be hard to be raised in the home of a hero. If your father or mother, brother or sister has made it big, it can make you feel like you have a whole heap of impossible expectations to live up to. Maybe that was Saul's story.

Rocketed to the top

The young leader's pathway to promotion was unbelievably speedy. Saul received a powerful prophecy and then just seven days later he was crowned king of Israel. Sounds great, doesn't it? No confused questioning of God to ask if He would ever fulfil His promises. No season of wondering if he was imagining the whole thing. Promotion landed on his lap. However, success only lasted for a season. He was a great leader - for about two years. Then things started to go wrong.

Instead of facing his flaws and seeking healing for his soul, Saul relied on the praises of people to build him up. I believe he lived with a constant need for recognition and respect. That's what life can be like without inner stability. Saul ended up giving in to opinions rather than obeying the voice of God. As a result, he never fulfilled his purpose. He lost everything. Saul looked like a success (as many of us do), but he had a host of insecurities that cost him his destiny. That's how important our hearts are. Proverbs 4:23 says: "Guard your heart for it determines the course of your life." (New Living Translation)

It's not our education or our upbringing that decides our future. It's not our gifts or talents that secure our success. It's our hearts that determine whether or not we fulfil our purpose. According to 1 Samuel 13:13, God would have given Saul an everlasting kingdom, but his craving for people's approval caused the Lord to find a new leader. The destiny that David stepped into was originally intended for Saul. Saul's heart issues cost him his purpose.

University of Adversity

The university of adversity is a painful place to be, but it produces phenomenal graduates. Going through your process can be unpleasant, yet it leads to maturity. However hard the path may be, the outcome is worth the wait. It is better to allow God to train you in the valley so that you are fit for your purpose on the mountain top. I don't know your story, but I know you've got one. What were your parents like, if you ever knew them? How was their marriage, if they ever tied the knot? How did you get on at school, if you were educated? Were you the popular kid or the butt of bullies' jokes? Did teachers encourage you or humiliate you? Are your siblings your best friends or your fiercest foes? Was growing up a bundle of joy or a nightmare that you are trying to forget? Or was it something in between?

Have you been blessed with wonderful relationships or have you been beaten up by betrayal? Has life surrounded you with happy surprises or overwhelmed you with disappointments? Perhaps your journey has been a mixed bag of joy and sadness, success and failure, ups and downs. What about your gifts and calling? Do you feel unfulfilled because your life isn't adding up to much? Perhaps you have inspirational dreams, but none of them seems to be coming to pass. Have you been in the same place doing the same things for far too long? Is life one big battle and you are desperate for a breakthrough?

Your life is your story. It is the catalogue of events which brought you to where you are now. It is tempting to try to distance yourself from difficult experiences. However, if you will surrender them to the Lord and ask Him to heal your soul, your struggles can become the stepping stones to your destiny. God has extraordinary things in store for you so He wants you to be ready when the time comes for your promotion. I heard Joyce Meyer say that, in her view, 90% of Christians never achieve their potential. I know that if you are reading this book, then you want to be in the ten per cent of believers that do fulfil their purpose. My mandate is to help you get there.

I have seen vast numbers of men and women step into their destiny as they allowed God to work on their hearts. At our two day retreat called Healed for Life, believers who ranged from the young and old and from veteran leaders to new converts have been restored after suffering hurts that they did not even know were hindering their lives. They left restored, refreshed and more ready than ever to fulfil their God-given destiny. Remember that it is your heart that will determine the course of your life. So can I suggest that you prioritize your inner well-being? Join me on a journey towards freedom, security and maturity.

Following in their footsteps

Who is your favorite Bible hero? Is it Abraham, the father of our faith; Joseph, the prisoner who became prime minister; David, the shepherd boy who led his nation? Perhaps you are drawn to Esther, the orphan who became a queen, or Paul, the apostle who wrote a third of the New Testament? What do all these Bible heroes have in common? There was a process of transformation that they needed to go through in order to be ready for their destiny. Very often, like our Bible heroes, we need to be perfected at the university of adversity so that we can handle the blessing.

Remember, Jesus came to give you life. Not a half-baked existence but a meaningful and enjoyable life. In the movies, unknown wannabe actors appear in films to make them look real. They are known as extras. They are not the main characters. In fact, they are not even the supporting actors. They just make scenes look genuine. They give a film depth so that the real stars can shine. God did not create any extras in life. You are not an extra. You are the leading lady or leading man of your life. He designed every one of us to make a difference. He planned you for a unique, important purpose. Only when you are working towards your God-given mission will you know true contentment. Nothing less satisfies.

God is amazing, He is powerful, He is able and He made you in His image. That means you have the potential to become great in God. You were designed on purpose with unique desires and skills to make an impact in the world around you. He wants to promote you, prosper you and use you to influence your generation.

This world needs brilliant educationalists who will inspire the young and talented musicians who can bring hope instead of fear. People need to meet conscientious cleaners who will shine for Jesus and compassionate carers who will reveal the Lord's love. We need excellent administrators, powerful preachers, mighty miracle workers, phenomenal business leaders, inspired movie makers and anointed doctors. The list could go on. It is God's desire to promote people who are full of the Holy Spirt and overflowing with His love. It is always better for His children to occupy positions of influence. However, He knows that you and I have to be ready - inside and out.

The devil's dirty tricks

The devil knows your infinite potential as a child of God so he makes it his mission to take you out of the game. If he can crush your confidence, drown you in self-pity or break your heart, he thinks he might prevent you from fulfilling your purpose. He wants to render you and I inactive and he uses disappointment, discouragement and defeat to do this dirty work. He lies to us, saying things like: "You will never see your promises come to pass" in the hope that you and I will give up on God.

Now here's the thing. The very calamity that satan planned for my destruction can become a training ground for my promotion. What the devil meant for your harm, God will use to hone your character if you surrender it to Him. There is nothing too traumatic or terrible that God cannot turn around to our advantage. When He says in Romans 8:28 that: "All things work together for good to those who love God and are called according to His purpose", He means *all* things. That is what makes the Lord different from us. He works miracles. On many occasions, we are the very miracles He has made.

I know that you have faced soul-destroying setbacks. I realize that you have felt untold pain and experienced problems that won't seem to go away. I wish it were not the case, but we live in a fallen world. The truth is that brothers will betray one another, friends will fail us and loved ones will let us down. So we need to know how to deal with devastating disappointments. When we discover how to be completely healed of all our pain, how to be released from all the burdens of the past, then our setbacks can become springboards instead of stumbling blocks.

Hope awakened

My Bible hero, Joseph, whose story is told in Genesis, suffered terribly in his lifetime. He was hated, betrayed, rejected and forgotten. Yet he rose out of 13 years of distress to fulfil his destiny. He found out how to be healed in the depths of his innermost being and he allowed the pain and pressure of slavery and imprisonment to became his process of transformation. By the time opportunity knocked, Joseph was ready and waiting at the door.

I believe that if you follow the 'Joseph Process' which is revealed in the chapters of this book, it will help to lead you through the doorway to your destiny. As you read, you will see yourself in the pages and discover things about yourself that you did not know. You will find out how to accelerate your transformation. Each chapter deals with a different heart issue that our hero Joseph grappled with on the way to fulfilment. They are the same issues that you and I need to face for the sake of our future. As you read, ask the Holy Spirit to pinpoint problems that have held you back and to show you how you can be free. You are en route to fulfilling your God-given purpose. This book can help to get you ready.

Prayer

Father God,

I ask You to take me on a journey of transformation as I read this book. Please help me to open up my heart to You as I read and I ask You to open my eyes to see what You see. Change me to be more like You, I pray. I want to be ready for my destiny so I ask You to do a deep work within and I ask You to help me to be patient while You change me. I rededicate my life to You today. Take me, mold me and make me into someone You can use for Your glory.

In Jesus' name, I pray,

Amen

Declarations

The Word of God is powerful and it changes us. I encourage you to take Bible verses that reflect what God is doing in you, personalize them and speak them over your life. Here are some examples of verses that could help you:

"The plans I have for you are plans to prosper you and not to harm you, plans to give you a hope and a future." Jeremiah 29:11

"I press on that I may lay hold of that for which Christ Jesus has also laid hold of me." Philippians 3:12

"Your kingdom come, Your will be done on earth as it is in heaven." Matthew 6:10

Chapter 2
JOSEPH'S JOURNEY

Joseph was a miracle child. His parents, Jacob and Rachel, had been trying for a baby for years. When a little boy eventually arrived, he was his mum and dad's delight. However, Joseph's family soon fell apart when his mother died giving birth to his younger brother, Benjamin. We don't know how old Joseph was when his mum passed away, but he was probably just a boy. Our parents are supposed to provide the scaffolding around our lives while we are growing up. So when our mother or father is suddenly taken away, it can be devastating. We miss their love, but we also lose the frame of our world.

Jacob had two wives. However, he only ever had eyes for Rachel. Joseph was the firstborn of Rachel, the woman he loved and lost. And Joseph came along when Jacob was getting on in years. Something about that combination caused him to love Joseph more than all his other children. Jacob didn't hide his favoritism. In fact, he flaunted it. Joseph was treated differently from the others. When the rest were out working, Joseph was at home relaxing. Worst of all for the others, their dad made an exquisite coat for his dearest son.

It is hard to be denied the love you deserve. Whether from parents or even a spouse, it can be terribly demeaning to be treated with indifference. When it comes from someone you live with, it is like a permanent cold shoulder. What makes it even harder is to see the one who should love you lavish their attention on another. If you have experienced that kind of rejection, it will be very important to embark on your own healing journey. This kind of pain is very often buried so you will need God's Spirit to shine His light into the hidden crevices of your heart.

A father's favoritism

Jennifer grew up in the shadow of her older, more intelligent brother. He excelled at school and university, attracting constant praise from their father. It's not that Jennifer was stupid. However, in comparison to her brilliant brother, she always felt like a let-down. As an adult, Jennifer constantly felt the need to prove herself to the people around her. She was very determined and worked long hours to secure rapid promotions as work. She saw herself as a successful Christian woman. At our two day retreat Healed for Life, God shined His light into her heart and she was brought back to memories of childhood. Jennifer always knew her parents loved her so she didn't realise how hurt she had been by her father's favoritism. God healed her soul and gave her a wonderful sense of her immense value. She left feeling secure. Jennifer continued to succeed at work, but no longer craved recognition.

It was this kind of painful favoritism that Joseph's brothers had to endure. To make matters worse, it would seem that Joseph had not yet been matured in love. He didn't think about his brothers' feelings. He did what many children do and bad-mouthed his siblings to his father, deepening the problems between he and his brothers. I don't think Joseph understood how hurtful the situation was for them. So when he saw a glimpse of his destiny, instead of downplaying his promise of prominence, he rubbed their noses in it and told the whole family about his dreams of grandeur. The others were incredulous. "So you think you're going to be the big boss, do you?" Envy and disdain soon turned to hatred.

11

Family in crisis

Jacob seemed oblivious to the fact that favoritism was slowly destroying his family. Jealousy and abhorrence are strong emotions and they always seek to harm the object of their attention. Poisonous passions were festering deep down in the hearts of the brothers. Difficult or dysfunctional relationships often appear alright to the outside world. That is partly what makes them so painful. Perhaps you were raised in a family where problems were buried. Maybe you have lived with a partner who could not handle the truth. When things simmer beneath the surface and everyone pretends that all is well, it can be unbearable.

Joseph's brothers eventually reached boiling point. The young men were working in the fields while Joseph was at home. Jacob sent Joseph to find out how the men were doing. Far from the glare of their father's eyes, the brothers grabbed the chance to blot out the bane of their lives. Their first thought was to kill him. They stripped Joseph of his tunic, the coat that reminded him how much his father loved him. They beat Joseph, kicked him and threw him into a pit. Then they sat down beside the cavernous hole and had a picnic. Joseph pleaded for mercy from the bottom of the pit, but they ignored his cries. He had no food, no water and no one to help. At just 17 years of age, Joseph's world was torn apart. His privileged life became a living hell.

Most people's lives are marked with one form of tragedy or another. Maybe someone you trusted turned on you, perhaps you were attacked by a stranger or abused by a so-called friend. It could be a terrible accident or the loss of a loved one. Trauma can choke the very life out of us. We can be branded by the betrayals that broke our hearts. Life-altering events can drain the color from our world and shatter our perceptions of the people around us. We try to return to normality, but everything has changed. We live our life in the shadow of those events. Time passes and we think we are fine. However, if something happens that takes us back, we experience moments of sadness. These are telltale signs that we still need more healing.

Sold as a common slave

Joseph's brothers saw some Ishmaelites riding by. They decided to make a bit of money and sold him as a slave. Joseph was taken to Egypt where he was bought by an influential businessman called Potiphar. I wonder how many times he relived that dreadful day. A toxic mix of grief and bitterness. From being his father's favorite to worse than a nobody, Joseph was now a common slave. It is horrible to be trapped in a pattern of reliving agonizing events. We can find ourselves going back over every detail, wondering what we could possibly have done differently. Sometimes we know exactly what we should have done differently and feel tormented.

Joseph's trauma changed everything. When he lived in the luxury and comfort of his own home, it was easy to imagine how his dreams might come to pass. But now, they must have seemed ridiculous. Completely alone, living in filth and squalor, Joseph was probably heartbroken. The desperation and rejection must have been crippling. He had to pull himself together if he wanted to survive. Joseph probably didn't even know how to work because at home he hardly lifted a finger. Now he had to learn fast. He did not want to attract the wrong kind of attention.

Trauma is debilitating. It can drain away your self-belief and totally incapacitate you. Jasmin is a minister from California. She suffered a terrible tragedy when her niece committed suicide. Jasmin was very close to the young woman so her untimely death was devastating. Jasmin was frozen by pain and tormented by confusion, but carried on as best she could. She came to Healed for Life to support a friend. Jasmin quickly realized that she herself needed every single session. When we dealt with grief, God did a miracle and healed her broken heart. Every question that had crowded her thoughts unraveled in the presence of God. She left restored, refreshed and re-energized. Shortly after she returned home, Jasmin's husband contacted the office to thank the team - explaining that he had got his wife back.

Despite desperate circumstances, Joseph worked hard. He made every effort to please his new master. As a result, he was quickly promoted to oversee his fellow servants. Unfortunately, Potiphar had an unfaithful wife who tried relentlessly to lure Joseph into bed. She wouldn't take no for an answer and eventually threw herself at her husband's servant. Joseph ran as fast as he could from temptation and snubbed the seductress. Furious, she screamed, seized his jacket and accused Joseph of rape. It was her word against his. False accusation can be crippling. The sense of incredulity that rises within and the agony of knowing that people all around you believe a lie can crush even a resilient Christian. Whether untruths are told about you or vicious rumors spread like fire, they can destroy relationships, families and even ministries.

Locked up

Joseph soon found himself locked up yet again. This time it was in the palace prison. Please don't imagine the comfort that Broadway musicals suggest. Psalm 105:18 tells us that he was shackled with fetters that injured his ankles and chains that bound his neck. Prison is terribly distressing at the best of times. To be behind bars without cause must be harrowing. Thoughts of injustice must have tormented him. However, I believe that the hope of his calling burned within. Despite his terrible plight, he was sure God's plans for his life still stood. During his darkest and most difficult season, again Joseph served diligently. This time he helped the prison officer. Soon he was promoted a second time - even while he was in jail.

No matter where you are or what you are going through, you can shine. Even in seasons of pain and pressure, you can exhibit uprightness and integrity. This will get you noticed - if not by man, then certainly by God. Don't wait for fulfilment to believe the Lord for a breakthrough. We can experience blessing even in the midst of the fiercest battle. Joseph was given responsibility in prison for overseeing the well-being of other inmates. When the king's butler and baker were thrown into jail, he got to know them. It wasn't long before they both had dreams which Joseph interpreted. Just as he predicted, the baker was beheaded and the butler was restored to royal service. This was just the break that Joseph had been waiting for. The butler promised to tell the authorities about his predicament once he was free. Joseph would be vindicated and released!

I can imagine that Joseph dreamed about his first few weeks of freedom. There must have been a spring in his step and a new song on his lips. He must have been thinking, "I knew God would come through for me. This is my moment..." But it wasn't. Hours turned into days, days turned into weeks and weeks turned into months. The butler forgot about Joseph. Have you ever been sure that your breakthrough was here? Everything was set for your promise to be fulfilled. Then nothing. After believing God for a husband or wife, the perfect partner walks away. After years of believing God for a baby, a late period points to menopause not pregnancy. After waiting for your business breakthrough or your door to open, what looked like the chance of a lifetime turned out to be a wild goose chase.

Forgotten, again

The cartoon world is the only place where disappointment is
funny. The coyote's dreams collapse as he disappears over the
cliff. The hunter misses his 'wabbit' one more time. In real life, it
can be crushing. Disappointment knocks at every one of our
doors. Just because it is common does not mean it is not desperately
difficult. It sits like a rock in our souls. All too often, it makes us
feel like giving up on our dreams. We feel humiliated and cheated.
That's why it is vital to learn how to deal with disappointment.

It is too easy to look to circumstances and feel despondent.
However, our God is the God who parted the Red Sea. With the
ocean in front and an army behind, things looked hopeless. Never
before in history had a sea separated. Yet our God did what man
could never have imagined was possible. He made a way where
there was no way. That same Lord of All has a thousand ways of
getting your answer to you. Joseph seemed to be back where he
started. He was in prison with no obvious way out. I am sure satan
was hoping Joseph would give up on God. The Bible says that
Abraham hoped against hope that he would have a baby in his old
age. He held on to his dream because God had promised. His great
grandson Joseph knew the hand of the Lord was upon his life so
he hoped when life looked hopeless and continued regardless.

One day...

Sometimes all God wants from us is that we carry on doing the
right things when we feel like falling apart. The first sign of
strength is the ability to continue. The more we do, the better we
feel and the more our faith starts to grow again. You never know
when breakthrough is just around the corner. Joseph did not know
if he would have to wait a day or a decade after the butler forgot
him. Despite the delay, he decided to stay strong. In the event, our

hero had to wait two more years. One day (which probably started like every other), Joseph was summoned to Pharaoh. His God-given gift for deciphering dreams was called upon by the king. Joseph bathed, shaved and exchanged prison overalls for smart new clothes, ready to be presented to Pharaoh.

The favor of the Lord surrounded Joseph as he revealed the meaning of the king's disturbing dreams. Egypt's leader was blown away by Joseph's wisdom and brilliance. Pharaoh instantly appointed him prime minister. Joseph woke up that historic morning in prison. By the evening, he was in the palace, poised to fulfil his purpose. During seven years of an abundant harvest, Joseph instigated the world's first tax system, holding back sufficient grain to feed the entire nation during the predicted drought. When severe famine hit the region, there was food available for everyone. Egypt and Israel were saved from starvation. Joseph accomplished his mission.

Prayer

Heavenly Father,

I know there is nothing too difficult for You. If You brought Joseph through 13 years of suffering, You can bring me through to victory. I ask You to speak to me through this man's life to encourage me in my breakthrough. I know You are faithful. I know You are able. So I pray that You would do the work within me so that when my day of destiny dawns, I am ready to arise. I surrender to the work of Your Spirit in my heart and life.

In the name of Jesus!

Amen

Chapter 3

YOUR INNER PICTURE

"Now Israel loved Joseph" Genesis 37:3

When I met my husband, I was in my final months of Bible School. He had just planted a church. As soon as we were married, I joined him in ministry. After graduating, I sought secular work while the church was still small. The favor of God opened doors and I was quickly promoted until I was running the communications division of Prince Charles's most prestigious charity. I was a wife, mother, pastor and vice president. Each role gave my life a sense of value. The titles and kudos that went with them built my confidence. They made me feel whole. The stage was set for success. Or was it?

My self-worth was based on what I did rather than on who I was. If I am really honest, it made me feel valuable to tell people I was a pastor. When I talked about my work for the Prince, it gave me a sense of importance. My identity was wrapped up in my roles. As a result, I was not stable. If my job makes me feel good about myself, what happens if I lose it? If being called 'Pastor' gives me value, how will I cope with the rejections of ministry? God wants our identity to be founded in His opinion of us, not man's. God would not raise me up on shaky foundations. He had to go to the root of my identity flaws. He revealed rejection deep within and showed me my insecurities. He uncovered old wounds so that He could heal me. He broke down my veneer in order to build the real me back up. It was a challenging journey, but it brought great transformation. Many of the healing programs we run today have originated from that process, bringing multitudes of men and women to their own place of peace and freedom.

Framed

Joseph's mum died when he was young and his brothers hated him. However, our hero always knew his father's affirming approval. From a tender age, Joseph understood that he was special. His dad lavished him with love. It is amazing how much stability can be instilled in the heart of a child when they know that their father believes in them. Our view of our earthly father nearly always frames our view of our heavenly Father. Put simply, we assume God is like our dad. If our father was distant, we assume God is somewhat detached from us. If our Pa was kind, we can believe that the Lord is too. Jacob helped Joseph develop both a sound identity and a positive picture of God, his Heavenly Father.

Betrayal and rejection met Joseph at every turn for what must have seemed like a lifetime. Yet the foundations of assurance were laid in his heart at a young age. He was a slave, but saw himself as a son. He was a prisoner, but he knew deep down that he was free. How do I know that? The Bible says in Proverbs 23:7 that: "As a man thinks in his heart, so is the man." In other words, it is impossible to rise beyond your situation if you believe you have got what you deserve. If you feel like a slave then you will behave like one and remain one. Not Joseph; he knew that his value was not determined by his circumstances. A strong sense of identity enabled him to rise up, even in the midst of affliction.

So what is identity?

Psychologists say that our identity is made up of three parts: our self-image, our self-esteem and our individuality. Your self-image is the picture that you have of yourself and it is quite resistant to change. Stop for a moment and answer the following question as honestly as you can. What do you believe that other people think about you? I'm talking about family or friends who know you pretty well. Jot down your first impressions on a piece of paper. This simple exercise is a rough indicator of your self-image. You can decide if you think that it is healthy. You may have a fairly good self-image, but you still struggle with low self-esteem.

Self-esteem is your evaluation of your worth. It is your judgment and your attitude about your value. Many issues can affect our judgement of ourselves. The words that were spoken to you by your parents, carers or even teachers will have influenced the value that you place on yourself. The way that you were treated by both peers and people in authority will have had a bearing on your assessment of your worth. Self-esteem encompasses beliefs like 'I am of great value' or 'I am not good enough' and emotions such as confidence or shame.

Individuality is the trickiest to explain. It is the sense of the importance of your own needs, desires or goals as opposed to those of other people. It is the belief that your unique aspirations deserve to be heard.

Servant

Noreen was sent to live with her wealthy aunt in eastern Nigeria when she was just seven. Her parents were in desperate poverty and believed that they were giving her a better future than they could offer. Noreen lived alongside her cousins, but was treated very differently to them. Forced to get up before dawn, she had to clean the house, cook and serve the family. Her cousins, on the other hand, would wake up to the hearty breakfast she had prepared and then get dressed for school. They would be educated while she would continue scrubbing floors. Leaving her aunt's house aged 16, Noreen eventually found her way to the UK. She married, had children and got a reasonable job. However, her self-esteem was in tatters and her individuality had been squashed. Deep inside, she saw herself as a servant: a little lower than everyone else. She was apologetic, shy and easily intimidated by assertive people.

As the Healed for Life team ministered to Noreen, the scales fell from her eyes and for the first time she understood why she felt the way she did. She believed that she was less important than everyone else. She felt like a doormat. Noreen poured out her pain before the Lord as He revealed the depth of His love for her. She began to realize that she was enormously precious to her Heavenly Father. Deep down inside she began to believe that she was wanted. As God healed her heart, her view of herself began to change. Now, Noreen is a strong, vibrant wife, mother and minister of the gospel. Her broken identity was restored as we ministered to her in the presence of God. She now sees herself as a valuable daughter of the Most High.

Too small

One of the most significant words I received was spoken over me at Bible College. I can't remember the topic being taught that day or why I had gone to the front of the auditorium for prayer. However, I will never forget what the Dean of Students pronounced as he prayed over me: "You're too small! You're too small in your own eyes." I can still hear those words like it was yesterday.

You know the story of the 12 spies. Their job was to glean information about Canaan and report back to Moses. Remember,

God had sworn that He would give them the land. He performed miracle after miracle delivering the Jewish people from Pharaoh and then provided for them in the desert. They knew from experience that God was both faithful and able. That was not enough. For God to use us, we must believe in Him. But we must also believe in ourselves. Ten of the twelve spies did not believe that *they* were able. I am certain that they knew that God was able yet could not conceive of the possibility of Him using them. It cost them (and the rest of their nation) 40 years of nomadic wandering. They saw themselves like insignificant insects: "The land through which we have gone as spies is a land that devours its inhabitants, and all the people whom we saw in it are men of great stature. There we saw the giants... and we were like grasshoppers in our own sight..." Numbers 13:32-33

When we have a diminished view of ourselves, all too often we will also have an inflated opinion of others. The spies first saw the inhabitants of the land as 'men of great stature' and soon convinced themselves that these people were 'giants'. The smaller we feel, the bigger we believe others to be. For example, I might be going for a job interview and start worrying that the other hopefuls are better qualified than me. Before too long, if I have a poor self-image, I may end up imagining that they can walk on water!

Your projector

When we have a dim view of ourselves, it will affect the way we carry ourselves and the opinion that others hold of us too. The verse above goes on to say that because the ten leaders saw themselves as insignificant insects, the inhabitants of the land saw them that way as well: "And so we were in their sight." Numbers 13:33b. Your self-image is like a projector. It conveys who you are to others. Proverbs 23:7 says: "As a man thinks in his heart so is the man." If you have a healthy identity, that will be relayed. However, if you feel inadequate or unimportant, that will be projected also.

The spies were supposed to be invading a foreign land, yet they believed their enemies were stronger than they were. They lost hope and caved in to fear. I doubt that invading a nation is on your agenda. Nonetheless, whether it is a business venture, a marriage proposal or a new ministry, your view of yourself will affect how you come across and how others respond. I had low self-esteem and a confused self-image. On one hand, I was a bag of insecurities and felt less important than other people - particularly those that I thought were impressive. On the other hand, I was full of self-importance. My buried feelings of inferiority were too painful to face so I derived a sense of superiority from my job titles and positions. God had to do a deep work to heal me and straighten out every crooked way. Eventually, my opinion of myself started to match God's view.

You may have a pretty healthy inner image and simply need a new injection of faith. Then again, as you read this perhaps you recognize that your self-image is in shreds and needs healing. Don't worry. God chooses the broken, fixes us and then sends us out to bring Him glory. He is a Master Restorer. Healed for Life exists to bring anyone who wants to become their best on a journey to genuine peace and freedom.

A marked identity

Our identity is molded throughout our lives but especially while we are growing up. We absorb the beliefs of those closest to us - both their opinions of the world and their assessment of our value. Then we either accept their perspectives or reject them. Either way, they will have affected who we think we are. At the same time, two powerful 'shapers' chip away at the sculpture that eventually becomes our identity: experiences and words. What happens to us affects our view of our worth and what is said to us penetrates our hearts.

God literally made mountains and stars by speaking and we were created in His image. The Bible says that death and life are in the power of the tongue. People can both harm and heal with words. Fleeting remarks can leave a lasting impact. What people say to us and about us often ends up shaping our understanding of ourselves.

When the truth is a lie

Rosemary grew up in a supportive Christian home. However, she was never told by either of her parents that they loved her just for who she was. She didn't know what it was like to be held in her dad's arms while he told her how wonderful she was. She never heard her mum mention all the reasons why she was wonderful. If Rosemary did well at school, she would be congratulated, but she was never celebrated just for being herself. She grew up in a vacuum of unconditional affirmation.

So when harsh words were spoken with authority by teachers, they penetrated her heart. "You will never amount to anything!" one teacher yelled at her when her math score was below average. "You're stupid!" another tutor bellowed in front of a class full of her peers. No-one had told Rosemary anything to contradict these words so they became her truth. She believed she was stupid and would never succeed. Rosemary got saved in her twenties and entered church leadership in her thirties. She served God faithfully, but always seemed to struggle with low self-worth. She had been through a lot of healing yet she was certainly not free.

Rosemary attended Healed for Life and the Spirit of Truth shined His light into her heart. Suddenly, she was reminded of these words. Although she had been aware of what these men had said, she had no idea that her entire identity had been branded by their cruel comments. She couldn't take compliments because they contradicted her "truth". She could not handle any negative feedback because it confirmed her low view of herself. She lacked confidence, struggled to like herself and was defensive.

She sobbed as she told God what her teachers had said. She was set free from the spirit of rejection and self-hatred. Rosemary then confessed the real truth of her ability and value over her life. The freedom she felt was phenomenal. A weight had been lifted and a peace released. For the first time in her life, Rosemary realized that she was like her Daddy God: smart and successful.

Names

We don't know much about Abraham's upbringing. His dad Terah clearly had his best interests at heart when he gave him a name. Abram means *'exalted father'*. Perhaps Terah had an inkling of the battle his son would fight to become a dad. Or maybe he had high expectations of him becoming a leader in their tribe. Whatever the reason, Terah did something good. The same is true for Sarah. She was also given a wonderful name by her parents. Sarai means ruler. Or to put it in 21st century language, manageress. The girl's parents were declaring leadership over her right from the start. Nevertheless, God had a problem with these names. They were good. However, His plans for this wonderful couple were great.

You may see yourself as relatively successful. Perhaps you think you've reached your ceiling. Maybe you believe that you're reasonably capable, yet you're not quite as gifted as other people. If your view of yourself is mediocre, it's time to get God's perspective. We are made in our Creator's image and He is the greatest.

God gave Abram a new name: Abraham, which means father of multitudes. The Lord knows the power of words. He knew that every time someone shouted to Abraham, they would be reminding him of his calling. To Sarai, God gave the name Sarah, which means queen. "No longer will people call you boss, now they will address you as queen." He was preparing them for their destiny.

How do you see yourself? Do you look at others and think they're more capable? Do you question your worth? The Lord is looking to take the lid off your limitations and show you your real value. You have often heard it said that good is the enemy of best. It is so true. Allow the Lord to paint a bigger picture of your purpose in your heart. Don't accept names or labels that will hold you back.

Rising above family expectations

Jacob had quite a different story to Abraham and Sarah. Right from the start, his dad spoke negative words over his life. Jacob means deceiver or usurper. Every time his father used his name, it was as though he was calling him a cheat. As he grew up, very little changed. His dad openly preferred his brother Esau. I believe that Jacob's identity was molded by a mixture of rejection and words. So it was not long before he was living his name and fulfilling his father's low expectations. He tricked Esau out of his birthright and then deceived his dad into giving him the firstborn's blessing that was rightfully his brother's.

Despite any shortcomings, God will never give up on us. Jacob messed up and went about things the wrong way, but the Lord was with Him through it all. During the years when I derived confidence from my gifts and talents, God in His kindness still used me and prospered me. His favor surrounds us, irrespective of our inner image. However, out of His kindness, He will often delay our promotion until our self-worth is good enough to be unchanged by success.

Peeling back the veneer

Jacob left home to start a family. He met Rachel (and Leah), married (twice) and had lots of destiny children. He became extremely successful and very wealthy. However, marriage, family, ministry and money will never heal a wounded heart. The day came when Jacob decided enough was enough. He got alone with God and made a decision: I am not leaving my prayer closet until something changes. After a night of wrestling in heart-wrenching prayer, God did not breathe fire from heaven. He did not release earth-quaking power. The Lord simply asked him his name. God, who created heaven and earth and knows everything, asked him what he was called.

Jacob's name symbolized the pain and failings of the past. It represented his dad's disdain and reminded him of the error of his ways. God was asking Jacob to acknowledge both his hurts and hindrances. The Lord never wants us to hide our wounds. He sent Jesus to heal them. We need to give God our pain in His presence by pouring out our hearts before Him like a child would to a loving mother. We need to tell our Lord what happened to us and how it hurt. As we release our pain, He pours out His healing balm.

Jacob faced the truth: he acknowledged his hurts and his mistakes. The Lord then made a new pronouncement over his son: "You will no longer be called Jacob, the rejected cheat. From now on you are Israel - Prince with God!" Our Heavenly Father gave him a new identity which was based on love and acceptance.

If you were to give yourself a name that relates to the way you see yourself, what would it be? If you were to imagine one word that sums up what you believe others think about you, what would that be? To be free from a limiting self-image or a damaged self-esteem, we need to face the truth. God wants to take us back to the place where our self-image was distorted, our self-esteem damaged or our individuality squashed: "In the very place where it was said to them, 'You are not my people,' there they will be called sons of the living God." Romans 9:25-26.

The Lord does not want us to pretend that bad things never happened to us. He calls us to acknowledge pain buried deep within so that He can take it away. He will not overlay a new identity on top of a wounded soul. He takes away the old in order to establish the new. He heals our hearts and then seeks to give us an identity based on our privileged position as dearly loved sons and daughters of the Most High God.

The forces of violence

Many different types of experiences affect us. One that can be particularly damaging is violence. There are often physical scars. However, the emotional scars are probably more serious. The enemy tries to use violence to mark us with fear and intimidation. Joseph's brothers did not just reject him, their behavior was brutal. He was attacked, stripped and thrown into a pit. I am certain that the teenager was traumatized by his experience. If you have ever been assaulted, it will be vital that you ask God to heal your heart and deliver you from its harmful effects. He knows the devastation it can cause. In fact, unconstrained violence was one of the reasons God gave for flooding the world and starting again through Noah (Genesis 6:11-12).

Jonathan, King Saul's son, was cut down to size by his dad's angry words: "You stupid son of a whore... do you think I don't know that you want him to be king in your place, shaming yourself and your mother?" (1 Samuel 20:30). Words hurt. In fact, the Bible likens them to piercing blows. Scripture goes on to say that Saul hurled his spear at Jonathan, intending to kill him. That must have been both frightening and heartbreaking. Jonathan must have wondered what on earth he had done to deserve such a devastating onslaught. He will probably have been left shaken and bruised. The effects of fierce anger can be debilitating if we don't deal with them. Sometimes when we suffer, we keep the memories locked away for fear of further pain or shame. Whether the violence is physical, verbal or sexual, it can be horribly destructive. Nonetheless, God is able to completely restore anyone who opens up fully and lets Him heal them.

Fury can overtake a person. It can change them in a moment and they become someone else - someone frightening: "Violence covers them like a garment" (Psalm 73:6). The relentless bombardment and rage can be soul-destroying for the people nearby who witness the behavior. The damage can go deep.

Living under a cloud of intimidation

Patrick and his sisters lived under a constant cloud of intimidation. Patrick's dream as a boy was to be a drummer. When his parents bought him a toy drum for his birthday, he was overjoyed. He sat on the stairs and played non-stop. The noise drove his father crazy, so just three days after he got his new gift, Patrick's dad snatched it, smashed it and hurled it out of the house. On several occasions, Patrick was punched in the face and beaten until he was blue.

By the time Patrick got saved in his late teens, he had been broken by his father's rage. He had a radical salvation and was deeply influenced by God's love, but he was not yet *fully* healed. Buried pain caused him to occasionally lash out at those he loved.

You see, if we don't deal with every source of sadness on the inside, all too often we find ourselves behaving just like those who hurt us the most.

With a strong healing anointing, God reached into the hidden places of Patrick's heart and finished the work that He had started many years earlier. What a joy it was to see such release and relief. Uncontrollable anger became a thing of the past and Patrick discovered a peace and freedom he had never before known.

God is our Healer and He is able to deliver both the attacker and the victim from all damage. David, who went through countless attacks, knew that when he talked to the Lord about his trials and asked for help, he would be set free: "He is my refuge, my savior, the one who saves me from violence." 2 Samuel 22:3 (New Living Translation) God is your protector and He can make you safe. He can also deliver you from painful memories so that they have no power over you. Talk to God as a child would to a kind and compassionate father. Then ask Him to heal your heart. Violence can mark a soul but the Lord can eradicate every trace and deliver us from all fear: "Violence shall no longer be heard in your land neither devastation nor destruction within your borders." Isaiah 60:18

A new identity

It is time for many of us to enjoy an exchange at the cross of Jesus. If your inner label has been *rejected*, bring that to the Lord and receive a new name: A*ccepted*. If you have seen yourself as a *disappointment*, give that to God and allow Him to call you *His delight*. If you have seen yourself as *second best*, allow the Lord to show you that you're *God's Choice*. Jesus paid for every contrary word and died for your wholeness, inside and out. If as you read, you realize that there are a lot of wounds within, I encourage you to come to Healed for Life - and keep coming until your inner image is sure and strong. Also, get hold of materials that will help to take you on a healing journey, such as my book, '30 Day Detox for your Soul'.

Perhaps you realize you have limited yourself. Maybe that is because you have been a victim of violence or intimidation. Whatever the reason, lay down any mediocre view of your potential and allow God to show you a picture of yourself - the way He sees you. Remember, you are made in the image of the Greatest and He has a significant plan for your life.

Prayer

Heavenly Father,

I come before you today just as I am. I open up my heart to You and ask You to heal me of those hurts that have affected the way I see myself. (Now tell the Lord about any experiences or words that have marked you. Ask Him to take the pain away and make you whole.) I bring every mediocre or negative word or label to You right now. (Now tell Him what words or labels you were given or that you have given yourself.) I receive your love afresh. I receive Your names for me: precious, accepted, wanted, able, significant, successful, loved. I ask You to take me on a journey to wholeness and I will not stop until the inner work is complete. I am your son/ daughter, I belong to You and I have a great future because You have made the way for me.

In Jesus' name I pray,

Amen

Declarations

The Word of God is powerful and it changes us. I encourage you to take Bible verses that reflect what God is doing in you and speak them over your life. Here are some examples of verses that might help you. I suggest that you personalize them by saying, for example: *"I am complete in Him"*.

"You are complete in Him who is the head of all principality and power." Colossians 2:10

"You can tell for sure that you are now fully adopted as his own children because God sent the Spirit of his Son into our lives crying out, 'Papa! Father!' Doesn't that privilege of intimate conversation with God make it plain that you are not a slave, but a child? And if you are a child, you're also an heir, with complete access to the inheritance." Galatians 4:6-7 (Message)

Chapter 4

THE MELTING POT

"He sent a man before them -
Joseph - who was sold as a slave.
They hurt his feet with fetters, he was laid in irons.
Until the time that his word came to pass."

Psalm 105:17-19

I rededicated my life to the Lord in my early twenties. Full of zeal, I shared the gospel at every opportunity with friends and strangers alike. I spent a lot of time each morning in prayer and the Word and gave up a promising career to go to Bible school. I started working for my church and served God with all my might. I thought I was ready for ministry. As I shared in chapter one, I was wrong.

The wear and tear of life had taken their toll on me. I was insecure around prominent people, worried about what others thought and I had an inflated view of myself. I was defensive when peers pointed out my shortcomings, hankered after the limelight and thought position was important. I wouldn't even allow my then husband-to-be to put a phone number on our wedding invitation because it wasn't the middle-class thing to do. I had no idea that these attitudes were all symptoms of problems deep within. In short, I had some serious issues.

We are called to show God's love to the people around us. We are mandated to be Christ's ambassadors here on earth. You and I represent Jesus. Our goal is to radiate His nature wherever we go. For that, our rough edges need to be made smooth. Where does that happen? In life's struggles. Every twist and turn acts like sand paper to make us more like the Lord whom we serve. The Bible says that Jesus learned obedience through the things that He *suffered*. The Son of God was led by the Spirit of God into the wilderness to be tempted. God deliberately subjected Himself to hardship, understanding that it is a vital tool in the development of human character.

I don't know how long you have been waiting for your breakthrough. I have not been on the road you have travelled and I don't know how hard it has been. I do know that God has not forsaken you. He is working all things together for your good. If you will allow Him, He will use every experience of your life, both good and bad, to prepare you for your destiny. Calamities and difficulties do not mean that God has forgotten His plans or His promises. The Bible says that God forgets our sins once we have confessed them. He chooses not to remember our wrong doing after we repent. He casts those memories into the sea of forgetfulness. However, He never forgets His promises and He never changes His mind: "The gifts and the calling of God are irrevocable." (Romans 11:29). The struggles and the wait don't mean that the promise won't come to pass. In fact, you will probably find that when you get your breakthrough, you value it all the more.

Seen it all before

I can't think of a Bible hero that didn't suffer on the way to success. David was told in his teens that he would become the king of Israel. At first, things seemed to go to plan. Not long after the prophetic word, David fought Goliath in front of the nation's warriors and delivered the giant's head to the king. He was spotted as a talented harpist and hired as King Saul's personal musician. He moved into the palace and became soulmates with the king's son, Jonathan. All was going well.

As David served King Saul with devotion, God gave him favor. He led armies to mighty victories and earned an impressive reputation. But his boss was insecure. The king could not handle someone else taking the limelight. Saul became consumed by jealousy. His love for the young warrior quickly turned to loathing and the king became hell-bent on killing his spiritual son.

Sometimes it looks like the stage has been set for our success. Everything is lining up for victory. Then it all goes horribly wrong. It can be soul-destroying to see perfectly crafted plans fall apart or promising signs evaporate into thin air. I believe that God likes to give us a taste of the future to help us endure difficulties. Your short-lived success was not a mistake. It was designed to give you the passion to press through until your promise comes to pass.

Hidden from the world

David spent the next ten years in exile, running for his life. He narrowly escaped many murder attempts. He slept rough and sheltered in the woods. The man he once called father hounded him day after day. Eventually, David found a cave where he and his followers could hide. It must have been dark and damp, but it provided shelter from danger. The name of that cave was Adullam. (1 Samuel 22:1). Most of us have our Adullams: the spot where our heavenly Father hides us while He is preparing us for His purposes. It is a place of difficulty. It is also a place of development.

Perhaps you feel as though nobody is noticing your gift. Maybe you have watched from the wings as friend after friend enjoys their breakthrough. Hang in there. God may well have you hidden while He is making final preparations. It is better to trust God and wait until you are ready than to step out ahead of time. David lived like a fugitive for a decade. He experienced rejection, hatred and betrayal. He must have wondered what had become of God's promises as he dwelt in a dirty cave instead of a royal palace. The Lord sent a motley crew of companions to the cave. Around 400 broken and bitter men gathered around David. I can guarantee that it was nearly as difficult living with these guys as it was escaping Saul! God was honing David's heart. He was preparing him to lead the nation.

David's position affected his whole family. Although they will have enjoyed the privileges that his early promotion provided, now they had to run for their lives too. The brothers who mocked him when he was 17 were now endangered for the sake of the brother they never really liked. Scripture says that they (probably unwillingly) joined David in Adullam's cave. Eventually, his family could not hack the life he lived and they abandoned him too: "I have become a stranger to my brothers and an alien to my mother's children..." (Psalm 69: 8). However, all the while he endured hardship and pain, the Lord was working on David's character to form a man so full of love and honor that he would become Israel's greatest king. Becoming great does not happen overnight.

Not disqualified

Jacob had a mighty call on his life, but his character was not ready for greatness. It all started at birth. His father Isaac called him Jacob because it means deceiver. So every time his father summoned him, it was like someone shouting: "Hey, cheat!"

Words run deep, especially when they are spoken by someone who has authority. Surely enough, Jacob started showing signs of deceit. He tricked his brother into selling him his birthright and then later robbed him of his firstborn's blessing. Jacob fled his home under a cloud of shame. In spite of his shortcomings, God had a great plan for his life. You may feel as though you have messed up one time too many. Perhaps you fall short every time you try to do the right thing. Maybe it is your prayer life or Bible study: you never finish what you start or keep to your commitments. You may keep falling into the same old sin, time after time. It is easy to think that our weaknesses disqualify us. However, we serve a God who is bigger than the things that are bigger than us.

The Lord has lifted me out of some terrible mistakes and helped me overcome many character flaws over the decades. He cleansed me when I saw myself as permanently soiled. He taught me how to consider the needs of others. And it's not just that. I don't know how many years it took me to establish a proper prayer life. I would set alarm clocks around my room and get friends to call me in the morning. However, as soon as the props were gone, I would slip back into oversleeping. It made me feel like a fraud. Christians are supposed to pray every day! It was the same with reading the Bible. I would start well, with ambitious reading plans. Then as soon as life got busy, it would all fall apart. By His Spirit, I got there in the end. All I had to do was to keep at it. Never stop trying. Every time you get up, you get stronger. You are closer today than you have ever been to your breakthrough. Statisticians tell us that the average smoker quits around twenty times before they successfully give up. They don't give up giving up!

God won't give up

God did not give up on Jacob and He won't give up on you. The Lord confirmed that He had a powerful plan for Jacob's life and then set to work on his character. God's plan for his transformation was a grueling job with his father-in-law, Laban. Jacob went through a painstaking process of laboring for a man who was craftier than he. God kept Jacob under Laban's thumb for 20 years while He chipped away at his character. "During the daytime, the drought consumed me, and the frost by night, and my sleep departed from my eyes. Thus I have been in your house twenty years; I served you fourteen years for your two daughters, and six years for your flock, and you have changed my wages ten times." (Genesis 31:40-41).

Perhaps you have a lying, cheating boss just like Jacob did. Maybe you are married to a hard-hearted husband like Abigail was in 1 Samuel 25. Perhaps you have been facing pressure for what seems like an eternity. God is able to use the hardship to get you ready for your future. As it says in Isaiah 48:10b: "I have tested you in the furnace of affliction."

You are not alone

Joseph went through terrible trials that lasted for 13 long years. He was hated, attacked, forced into slavery, falsely accused, imprisoned and forgotten. Nonetheless, one thing was clear through it all: "The Lord was with Joseph" (Genesis 40:21). All too often we think God has abandoned us. We wonder why He has left us in the wilderness and why He has forgotten His promises. Like the disciples, when the storm rages, we wonder if Jesus is really bothered about us. "Teacher, do You not care that we are perishing?" (Mark 4:38).

However tough it gets, remember that your heavenly Father *is* with you. Just as Jesus was with the disciples during the storm, so the Holy Spirit is with you through every valley and wilderness.

He will never leave you nor forsake you. I believe that the assurance that God was by his side kept Joseph going and it can keep you going too. He who has promised is faithful and will see you through.

We could do a 'before' and 'after' sketch of Joseph. Before suffering, you could be forgiven for describing him as self-absorbed, insensitive and arrogant. After affliction, he was wise, considerate and kind. He was transformed through fiery trial and tribulation. The pain of the process produced a man of great character and maturity who could lead a nation through famine.

It wasn't just Joseph who needed a process to perfect his character. God used the years of remorse and regret to do a work in his brothers too. After all, they had mighty destinies to fulfil and needed to become men who could carry the anointing and lead their tribes. The very same Judah who suggested they sell Joseph and profit out of his calamity offered to ransom himself for Benjamin 22 years later (Genesis 43:9). He was a different man. Life changed him into an honorable and selfless person: someone God could use.

It's for my good

It's easy to assume that every adversity is initiated in hell. However, God sometimes produces pressure to perfect His work in us: "God led you all the way these forty years in the wilderness, to humble you and test you, to know what was in your heart, whether you would keep His commandments or not." Deuteronomy 8:2. God actually created the wilderness experience to test and train His people. Year after year, they cried out to Him to deliver them from the very place where He had put them.

Some time ago, my husband and I were going through a barren season. We were running very fast in life and ministry in order to stand very still. There had been grand prophecies over our church and yet all we could see was people leaving in dribs and drabs. We would go to the nations and watch God move by His Spirit. Then we would come home to the harsh reality of a diminishing congregation. We had been through storms before, but this was different. We could not put our finger on the reason why people were leaving. Nothing big had happened. No-one was trying to split the church. No-one was accusing us of bad behavior. Folk were just voting with their feet. It was soul-destroying.

At that time, I contacted my mentor and asked if she had any wisdom to offer. When I saw her response, one word jumped out before I had the chance to read the message. It was *process*. I sighed, but at the same time felt relieved. This period was part of God's plan for our preparation. My job was to keep my heart soft and stay strong in faith throughout.

2 Corinthians 4:17 says: "Our light affliction... is working for us..." When someone works for me, they are charged with fulfilling my requirements. This verse says that pain and pressure actually work for us and not against us. Trials transform us. They can mold our character so that we become more useful to our Father. God uses difficulty, delay and disappointment to get us ready for destiny. He uses hardship to build resilience and maturity deep within. He uses the strains of a difficult life to prepare us for the abundant life. The more we surrender and allow the work within, the sooner we will find our way out. I will say it again: it's the *process* that produces the person that can possess the promise.

Prayer

Heavenly Father,

I am so grateful that You are at work in my life. I surrender to You and I ask You to mold me into Your likeness. Deal with anything in my character that is preventing me from fulfilling my destiny. Remove every obstacle in me that is slowing the flow of your love through me. I embrace the process of transformation and ask You for a quick work within. Thank you that You are with me every step of the way. You have not forsaken me. You have not forgotten me. Every plan and purpose will come to pass. Your promises to me will be fulfilled in your perfect timing. I trust You, I love You and I surrender.

In Jesus' name,

Amen

Declarations

The Word of God is powerful and it changes us. I encourage you to take Bible verses that reflect what God is doing in you and speak them over your life. Here are some examples of verses that could help you:

"For our present troubles... produce for us a glory that vastly outweighs them and will last forever!" 2 Corinthians 4:17

"But we... are being transformed... from glory to glory, by the Spirit of the Lord." 2 Corinthians 3:18

"Consider it pure joy my brothers whenever you face trials of many kinds, knowing that the testing of your faith produces perseverance and perseverance must finish its work so that you may be mature and complete not lacking anything." James 1:2-3 (New International Version)

Chapter 5

THE WAIT

"Joseph was thirty years old when
he stood before Pharaoh" Genesis 41:46

Our hero was a teenager when God first showed him his future.
Full of promise and hope, the 17 year old was delighted by his
dreams of grandeur. Something inside told him these were
heaven-sent pictures of his potential. I'm sure Joseph imagined it
would all come to pass quite quickly. Maybe not immediately
but soon. In reality, Joseph had to wait 13 long years for his
breakthrough. Then the dreams themselves - of his brothers
bowing down before him - were not fulfilled until he was 39
years of age. That was 22 years after he first heard from heaven.

Abraham and Sarah were already old when God promised them a
baby. In fact, Abraham was 75 when God first told him that his
descendants would own the land where he lived. I think we can
assume that Abraham expected God to act fast. It wasn't just that
his body was ageing. Sarah was getting on a bit too! However,
the father of faith and his wife had to wait 25 years for their
prophecy to be fulfilled. I wonder how many times Sarah cried
out to God. Most women have a strong yearning to use their
baby-making machines. The unfulfilled longing for a little one
can be heartbreaking. For ladies in biblical times it was even
worse. Folk assumed that barrenness was the consequence of
wickedness. People probably mocked her and judged her heart.

It must have been hard for Abraham to see Sarah suffer. He had his own issues to contend with too. As months turned into years and years merged into decades, he probably wondered if he had really heard God. Perhaps doubt tried to creep in and convince him that he was deluded about ever having any descendants. 25 years is a long time to wait. Although his name must have encouraged him, maybe there were moments when it made him feel like a fraud or a fool. I would not be surprised if his friends thought he was crazy. After all, nothing like this had happened before. Keeping on hoping must have been so hard.

Exam time

I believe that time is a test that we all have to take. So often our human instinct is to say: 'This is ridiculous. I've been waiting for far too long. I'm going to forget about the whole thing.' However, we need to learn to be patient. That does not mean that waiting is easy, but it is often very necessary. And it is something that everyone has to experience. Take heart. You are not alone and He who promised is faithful. The Bible says that after Abraham patiently endured, he received the promise. Against all odds, Sarah gave birth to a bouncing baby boy. Abraham was a dad at last.

There are many subsequent examples of other miracle babies who were also born after decades of delay. Isaac endured 20 years before his wife Rebekah conceived twins! Physicians thought Elizabeth would never have children, but she got pregnant when she was an old lady and gave birth to John who became the Baptist. Very often, the most precious presents from God take their time. Yet when they arrive, we value them more than words can say.

Hannah cried out for what must have seemed like a lifetime before Samuel - one of the greatest prophets that walked the earth - arrived. She went through years of disappointment and ridicule while she waited for the Lord to give her a baby. Yes, her husband loved her, but her dream was to be a mother. God had phenomenal plans for Hannah. He wanted to give her a son who would shake the nations. However, the Lord needed Hannah to become a woman who was capable of carrying a destiny child. God allowed the years of delay to perfect a work in her. When she promised to give God her dream baby, the Lord knew she was ready. It was the process that produced a person who could possess a mighty promise: "So it came to pass *in the process of time* that Hannah conceived and bore a son." (1 Samuel 1:20)

Setbacks

Along with eleven other leaders, Caleb was chosen to represent the tribe of Judah in spying out the promised land. He saw the giants that occupied it, but he knew that God was well able to give him and his countrymen the victory. Unfortunately, his ten fellow leaders were overwhelmed by doubt and fear. The result? God delayed the date for the conquest of Canaan. Everything that Caleb had been waiting for was put on hold. Not for a month or even a decade, but for forty years. Caleb was in his prime and would now have to wait until he was an old man to possess his promise. Like the rest of Israel, I'm sure he was grieved by the stratospheric setback. Nevertheless, he dealt with the disappointment and instead focused on God's faithfulness. How do I know that? Forty years later, he was still full of faith and as strong as he had been on the day he first spied the land. We can't stay strong when we're weighed down by discouragement. God gave Caleb a promise and he believed it.

Perhaps, like Caleb, the actions of others have brought your world crashing down around you. Maybe you have been betrayed. It is important to shift your focus from the mistakes of men to the power of God. However, in order to be able to look forward, we need to make sure we have dealt with the past. If things have gone horribly wrong for you, you will probably need to be healed. When dreams are dashed or terribly delayed, it can feel like a form of grief. We can't just sweep such disappointments under the carpet. We need to pour them out in prayer in the presence of God. I don't imagine that many people have been waiting 40 years like Caleb. I do know that however long it has taken, God's promises still stand. Everything around us may fall apart, but God's Word remains true: "The grass withers, the flower fades, but the word of our God stands forever." (Isaiah 40:8)

Wait on purpose

So what do we do while time is passing? This is a key. We wait *with* faith. Keep God's promise alive in your heart. Try not to think about human limits, but about God's infinite power. He could have given Abraham a baby when he was a young man, but the Lord wanted to show His greatness and teach us faith and patience. Picture your promise fulfilled. See yourself already living the dream. Imagine that wedding or that baby that God has given you His word about. See yourself preaching or running that business. You and I don't know how the Lord will do it, so we must not worry about the mechanics. That's God's job. Just believe. And remember, you are one day closer today than you were yesterday. Don't let go or give up on God's plans for your life. Fulfilment may be just around the corner.

In the twinkle of an eye

In the year 2000, tragedy hit our home when we lost our two-year-old little girl. Naomi, who was our only child at the time,

DOORWAY TO YOUR DESTINY

died very suddenly as a result of overwhelming septicemia. After she died, one of the things that saddened my husband and I the most was the thought of being apart from her for so long. We knew that we would see her in heaven, but that felt like a very long time to wait. Then God opened our eyes to His word. The Bible says that to the Lord, a thousand years is like a day and a day is like a thousand years. We did the math and realized that in heaven's scheme of things, we would see our sweet daughter in about 45 minutes. It was amazingly reassuring.

Sometimes time seems to pass very slowly, especially when we are waiting for our breakthrough. Yet, when we reach the other side and look back, a decade can feel like a matter of months. I want to encourage you. God's promises will be fulfilled in the fullness of time. Try to take your eyes off the ticking clock and instead determine to trust that your answer is around the corner.

Recently, I was talking to the Lord about some of my five year goals. It dawned on me what age my children would be when that period was over. Soon, my eagerness settled down. I did not want to wish time away. I encourage you to embrace the season of preparation that you are in. Enjoy your life now, thanking God for every good gift He has already given you. Fulfilment will come upon you before you know it so make every moment count. Rejoice in the season that you are in and keep a glad heart. Believe for better, but be grateful for what you have and for what the Lord is doing for you right now.

While we wait

We saw in chapter 3 that God had big plans for Jacob. The Lord picked this very fallible fellow to father His people and even named the entire nation after him. Because of the size of the calling, the Lord had a lot of work to do to make him fit for purpose. For twenty years, Jacob worked for a crook. Laban, his boss and father-in-law, constantly moved the goalposts, made him marry the wrong daughter, changed his wages without notice and generally behaved without any integrity. God was using this difficult season to work on Jacob's character. However, what really blesses me about this story is what God was doing *behind* the scenes *for* Jacob while He was working *on* Jacob.

As a young man, Jacob tricked his older twin Esau into giving up his birthright and later he stole his firstborn's blessing. So when Jacob left home, Esau hated him and was hell-bent on killing his brother. It was with trepidation decades later that Jacob returned to the land of Canaan to face his twin. Jacob was seemingly going from the frying pan to the fire. He left his father-in-law and brutal boss Laban, but was heading home to the hatred of Esau. It was at this time that Jacob had a life-changing encounter with the Lord.

Perhaps it feels like your situation is hopeless. Maybe you are surrounded by problem people or facing disheartening, even soul-destroying circumstances. There is no place like God's presence. Jacob determined that he would not let go of God until He touched his life afresh. So Jacob sent his family away and spent a whole night alone with the Lord. It was at the end of this night of prayer that God released a monumental blessing over his son. Jacob was given a new name, Israel. His old name represented his old nature and his old life. The new name marked a new beginning. The process of transformation in Jacob was nearly complete.

The power of an encounter

If you are downhearted, you need your own encounter with God. Tell Him the truth just like Jacob did. Pour out your heart like

DOORWAY TO YOUR DESTINY

water before the face of the Lord. Explain why you're disheartened. Disappointment can weigh us down if we don't deal with it. If life has dealt you some painful blows then I encourage you to come to Him in prayer. Tell God how low you feel, then give him every disappointment one by one. Leave them with Him and ask Him to fill you afresh. As our ministry grew, we realized the importance of regular refreshers in the presence of God. Many people return to Healed for Life again and again to allow God to renew and revive. Just as our cars need a regular service, so our souls go through many ups and downs and need time for repair and restoration.

God did a deep work on Jacob's character through a combination of hardship and encounter. Yet he still had to go home and face Esau. The last time Jacob saw his brother, Esau was enraged. Esau was not a particularly God-fearing man. He seemed to be more interested in his dinner than his destiny and in pleasing people than pleasing God. It can be hard enough for good people to change, but a man like Esau? The Bible tells us that bitterness poisons those who harbor it so there was every chance that Jacob's older brother had become more murderous than ever.

Have you ever looked at your life and wondered how God could possibly solve your problems? Where on earth is my spouse going to come from? There are a billion beautiful ladies in our church and no men! How am I ever going to find a wife when I get intimidated every time I try to talk to a girl? How am I going to get a job? I'm surrounded by highly skilled graduates who can't get work, who is ever going to employ me? I know I'm supposed to be preaching to the nations, but my own family won't even listen.

Behind the scenes

Jacob was so scared about seeing Esau that he sent servants with presents ahead of him to soften the blow. But Jacob could not have dreamt up what actually happened. While God was changing Jacob, he was also working on Esau. The Lord miraculously tenderized the heart of this once angry man who then welcomed his brother back home with open arms. God did what Jacob could never have done. The miracle doesn't end there. Esau then willingly surrendered the land of Canaan to his younger sibling and offered to leave to make room for Jacob and his family!

What is impossible with man is possible with God. You have no idea what God is doing behind the scenes of your life. There may be people who He is already prompting to offer you a promotion. There may be a healing that He is already working in your physical body without your knowledge. There may be doors that He is unlocking, ready for you to open. While we wait in faith, allowing God to work on us, He is making the way where there was no way.

The best prayer we can pray is not, "Do it now!" It is better to ask the Lord to get you ready for His purposes as quickly as possible. That is a cry of surrender and trust. Remember that God is your father and He has your best interests at heart. The devil wants you to believe that you have been forgotten and forsaken, but that is a lie. The One who promised is always faithful, never forgets and delivers at the right time. You have heard it said that He is never late. That is true. However, what we need to understand is that He is rarely early. He will come through in His perfect time.

Prayer

Heavenly Father,

I have been waiting for a long time. I really believed I would have received my breakthrough by now, but I am still waiting. I have felt down and disheartened. I am fed up of being let down at nearly every turn. I bring You every source of disappointment **(Now tell the Lord exactly how you feel and what has discouraged you the most. Be specific and then see yourself giving every setback to Him)**. I ask that You will fill me afresh with Your Spirit.

I know that You are faithful. I believe that You will do everything that You have promised to do. Give me the patience and strength to wait for Your timing. I want to be ready for my destiny so I'm willing to wait. I trust You. I thank You that You have my best interests at heart. Thank You because I know You are at work behind the scenes of my life. I will hold on to Your promises until they come to pass. I pray that You will prepare me and get me ready to fulfil my highest purpose.

I thank You for all the good things that You have already done for me. I thank You for this wonderful season of learning and growth. And I thank You for all the great things that You are about to do!

In Jesus' name,

Amen

Declarations

Remember, the Word of God is powerful and it changes us. Take these Bible verses and speak them over your life:

"Let us hold fast the confession of our hope without wavering, for He who promised is faithful." Hebrews 10:23

"The grass withers, the flower fades, but the word of our God stands forever." Isaiah 40:8

"You have made the heavens and the earth by Your great power and outstretched arm. There is nothing too hard for You!" Jeremiah 32:17

"He who has begun a good work in you will complete it." Philippians 1:6

Chapter 6

MY LOT

"They took him and cast him into a pit.
And the pit was empty; there was no water in it"
Genesis 37:24

I don't know what you have gone through. However, I do know that satan seeks to persuade you that your suffering and struggles have set you apart. It is almost like you hear whispering in your ear convincing you that your past separates you from other people. In the years after my daughter died, I saw myself as a survivor. Someone who had been to hell and back, and made it out alive. The tragedy defined me. I believed that I deserved extra compassion because of the loss I had suffered. When times were tough, I expected special concessions. When life was good, I saw myself as a hero for being happy. Most of all, I saw myself as different.

As I went on to have more children, this mindset continued. When I stood at the school gates waiting for my son to finish lessons, I thought of myself as the bereaved mum. Others had normal stories, but I had lost my little girl. I was always aware of the people who I had told and those I hadn't. It was an unspoken yet ever-present issue. It was my elephant in the room.

Victim at heart

It was not just that our first child died. Although our son was perfectly healthy, our second daughter suffered a great deal. Abby was born with her umbilical cord wrapped twice around her neck. She had been starved of oxygen for ten minutes with no detectable heartbeat. Abby spent the first ten days of her life in intensive care. Within two days of getting home from hospital, other problems emerged and she was readmitted. Our daughter endured about fifteen surgeries by the time she was six. Painful medical procedures became a normal part of her life and she faced daily challenges.

I did not just see myself as a grief-stricken parent. I was a victim mother with two difficult stories. When we see ourselves as different, we make allowances for all sorts of things. We accept isolation, allow negative thinking and excuse bad behavior. When we believe our lives are unusual, we can think that we can't achieve the breakthroughs that others enjoy. Self-pity can leave us feeling hard done by, disappointed and dejected. It does not create an atmosphere for faith or determination. It makes us feel like downing tools and giving up. Left unchecked, self-pity is a destiny destroyer. It devours your soul and causes its victims to be preoccupied with themselves.

Marked by life

My identity had become marked by tragedy and I felt I should be treated differently. I expected God to answer my prayers because He owed me some sort of consolation prize. This is not a place of faith, nor a platform for any kind of promotion. As a result, God in His mercy ministered to my heart. I had a life-changing encounter in His presence. I saw myself standing before the Lord with two toddlers in my arms (my girls) and one child at my feet (my boy).

I sensed God telling me to take Naomi - our child who died - into my arms and give her a big hug. I did so. Then, in my mind's eye, I handed her into the arms of my Heavenly Father. Next, I held Abby in my arms. I gave her a tight hug and I transferred her into God's hands. Finally, I picked up my little boy Benjy. I cuddled him and then placed him into God's care. As I entrusted my children to the Lord, I surrendered my identity as a victim mother. Just as you would remove a coat, I took off self-pity. In that moment, I knew who I was. Not a disadvantaged mother, but a dearly treasured daughter of the Most High. I no longer clung to excuses and I stopped wanting sympathy. I felt fulfilled just from knowing that I was favored by my Daddy God.

Tough times

Joseph must have been tempted to feel sorry for himself, and with good reason. He was betrayed, beaten, enslaved and imprisoned. Imagine how many times he must have felt like giving up on God. After all, it looked like God had given up on him. How often must he have felt like forsaking his dreams? They must have seemed like a joke as he swept the floors in Potiphar's house. Weeks, months and years passed him by. Just when promotion out of slavery seemed a possibility, he was accused of rape and thrown into prison.

After several years inside, he thought escape was certain when he gave an accurate prophetic word to a palace worker. Unfortunately, his ticket to freedom (the butler) neglected to plead his case: "Yet the chief butler did not remember Joseph but forgot him." Genesis 39:23. It is not just that the king's servant didn't remember. He completely forgot about Joseph. No doubt the enemy tried to push Joseph into depression. As a result of the butler's neglect, Joseph spent another two years in prison. That is a long time.

Feeling forgotten

How many times do we look at the delays and disappointments of our lives and feel forgotten? If the enemy can keep us thinking that we have been forsaken, he can trap us in our misery. Self-pity is a common human reaction to pain and hardship. We think we have been short-changed. We believe that we have had more than our fair share of struggles. It makes us focus on ourselves and our problems. Although the great patriarch Job had every right to feel dejected, it never helped him. He not only felt sorry for himself, he also hankered after the sympathy of others: "Have pity on me, have pity on me, O you my friends, for the hand of God has struck me!" Job 19:21

Sometimes we just want people to acknowledge the cruelty of our lives. It was only when Job took his eyes off his terrible troubles and instead reminded himself of the genuine goodness and greatness of God that his circumstances started to change. Self-pity nearly killed Jonah. He resented the Lord showing mercy on the people of Nineveh. Their undeserved blessing somehow made him feel robbed. Does that sound familiar? He was grieved when he witnessed God showing favor to unworthy sinners. He could not handle the kindness of the Lord because it did not seem fair. Jonah soon sank into despondency. He actually wanted to end his life: "It is better for me to die than to live." (Jonah 4:8)

My nation, Great Britain, is obsessed with fairness. This is positive when it's about ensuring that the poorest people receive support. It can be a problem, though. When we start to measure ourselves against others to determine whether we should be content, it becomes a real issue. When a sister in church being promoted sooner than me makes me feel badly done by, it could delay, or even completely abort, my breakthrough. Because God blesses a brother, it does not mean He loves me less. Until I can rejoice in someone else's season of blessing, I am probably not ready for my own breakthrough. The Lord has a unique plan for each one of us. That means different things will happen at different times and for different purposes.

At last!

My husband, Paul, was an expert in self-pity. There were times when he felt that the whole world was on top of him for weeks on end and no one was on his side. If people let him down, he felt sorry for himself. If money was tight, he felt wronged. If I messed up, he felt I was against him too! One day he was reading a book about how the enemy seeks to oppress believers. He looked up at me and said, 'God just told me that I suffer from self-pity."

'At last!' I shouted. 'It has dogged you for as long as I've known you and crippled you on numerous occasions." That very moment he vowed to the Lord that he would not allow it to nest in his life any longer. He went to the Lord in prayer and repented. He chose to shut the door on behavioral patterns that had dogged him for years. No more shutting down or blaming everyone else. No more sulking when times were tough. The change was amazing. He has been a happier, stronger and more resilient man ever since.

I love the story that the brilliant Welsh pastor Wynne Lewis used to tell. Soon after Wynne took over the leadership of a growing church in London, a man would stand up in service after service and cry out: "Woe is me for I am undone!" After a few weeks, the pastor got fed up. The next time the fellow repeated his mantra for all to hear, Wynne retorted from the pulpit in his wonderful Welsh accent: "Well do yourself up, boyo!" We have to fight self-pity like we would battle any other spiritual enemy. It is cruelly tempting to drown in our own sorry circumstances. However, it only ever keeps us from rising up in faith and victory.

It's not about me

Paul the apostle was whipped, beaten with rods, stoned, shipwrecked and imprisoned. He was deprived of sleep, food and water. He lived without basic comforts. Nevertheless, he showed amazing resilience. By keeping mission-minded, he seemed to save himself from self-pity. He wasn't focused on fulfilling *his* dreams. He was determined to accomplish God's purpose. Of course, we would hope that our dreams *are* God's purposes! A slight shift in emphasis means we can endure suffering and setbacks without being distressed. When we live to serve Christ no matter what the cost or discomfort, it will help to deliver us from self-pity.

The same Paul who suffered beyond measure told the Philippian Christians to rejoice in the Lord all the time! Not just when times were good, but when life was tough. He was clearly preaching what he practiced. Nearly every letter he wrote was full of thanksgiving and praise. This man would not allow his circumstances to steal his joy.

It is all too easy to assume that spiritual people don't stumble - that somehow they never go through anything challenging. That's not true. The Bible says that the righteous *do* fall, up to seven times a day! What makes them different is that they get back up afterwards. Self-pity weakens even strong people. In contrast, when we take our eyes off ourselves and look to God, He gives us the strength to stand: "Though the righteous fall seven times, they rise again..." Proverbs 24:16

When we choose, like Abraham, to hope against hope we will find the strength to arise out of discouragement. Self-pity opposes two of the most important attributes that we need to nurture within: faith and thanksgiving. You see, it is almost impossible to be filled with gratitude *and* self-pity. It is very difficult to be strong in faith while feeling sorry for ourselves. Thanksgiving is the gateway to God's presence and faith is the currency of His kingdom. Let faith arise from deep within. Stop and say some heartfelt thank yous right now to your Heavenly Father who loves you.

A common problem

The Bible clearly teaches that each one of us is unique. God has a tailored plan for your life that reflects your individual design. At the same time, one of the core lessons of Ecclesiastes is that nothing we go through is new: 'That which has been is what will be, that which is done is what will be done, and there is nothing new under the sun. Is there anything of which it may be said, "See, this is new"? It has already been in ancient times before us.' (Ecclesiastes 1:9-10)

I find the final scenes of Elijah's life sad. After one of the most extraordinary victories on Mount Carmel, defeating the prophets of Baal and proving the power of God, Elijah ran away, terrified of Jezebel. He escaped to a cave whilst displaying some telltale signs of self-pity. When we feel sorry for ourselves, we often want to retreat and hide somewhere where we can wallow in our circumstances. We believe the lie that our pain is unique or our circumstances are the worst.

Elijah bemoaned the fact that he was the only servant of God alive. Yet the Bible states that there were 7,000 men and women who maintained their faith in the Lord. Believing that he alone was left, Elijah told the Lord that he wanted to die. Self-pity always seeks to make us give up. It was at this point that God called time on this mighty man of God and raised up Elisha in his place.

History regularly repeats itself. Countless couples across the world have lost their children to untimely death. Indeed, many have lost entire families. Scores of parents have suffered like me and come out strong. Others have endured battles that are similar to yours and emerged successfully on the other side. Every test or trial has been faced by others down through the centuries: "The temptations in your life are no different from what others experience..." 1 Corinthians 10:13 (New Living Translation).

The Greek word for temptation here is the same as the one for trial. What you and I have experienced has been endured by umpteen others the world over. When we realize that our struggle is not all that different from the battles that others have had to fight, it can help us to put our lives into some sort of perspective. If we take our eyes off our individual issues and instead look to the greatness of God, the Lord can start to work within.

Rejoice anyway!

Isaac found a way of fighting discouragement. As he attempted to secure a source of drinking water for himself and his family, his efforts were thwarted again and again. Every time he broke through and dug a new well, the enemy took over. It would have been very easy for Isaac to feel defeated. Instead, he rose up, moved on and started again. He refused to allow failure and disappointment to keep him down. He was a happy man. Sometimes we need a little help to get to where Isaac was. The sludge of life can somehow block the well of joy that God wants to give us.

When we rejoice, it releases joy deep within. The joy of the Lord is our strength and when we rejoice we liberate the inner strength to rise above our circumstances. The name Isaac means laughter. I believe he learned to laugh at a very young age so he knew what to do as an adult when things got tough! Proverbs 17:22 teaches us that a merry heart does us good, just like medicine. I can be very serious so I am glad that God has given me a witty husband, a hilarious spiritual mother and a wonderfully funny covenant friend. Laughter does you good. Find someone who can help you let it out. I'm not funny, but thankfully they make up for it.

The benefits of breaking self-pity

When we feel sorry for ourselves, we are much less aware of the issues of others. Even while he was in jail, Joseph looked out for the well-being of his fellow prisoners. One morning he noticed that two inmates looked forlorn. They were not screaming or shouting. They just seemed sad. If Joseph had been focusing on his own affairs, he probably would not have noticed. His concern prompted him to question them. Soon the butler and the baker told Joseph about their disturbing dreams. Joseph explained what they meant and every detail came to pass. About two years later, it was the butler who informed Pharaoh about the interpreter in prison. Self-pity may well have kept Joseph in prison. Compassion for others paved the way for his monumental promotion. This can be a major key to your breakthrough.

Prayer

Heavenly Father,

I thank You for Your wonderful love for me. You have my life in the palm of Your hand. I am grateful for every good gift that you have given me. From the depths of my heart, I want to thank You. (Now tell the Lord, with all sincerity, what you are grateful to Him for. Thank Him for the times He has blessed you and protected you. Be specific.)

I am sorry for the times when I have felt sorry for myself. I have wallowed in my own issues and allowed self-pity to fill my soul for too long. I repent and I ask You to help me rid myself of it completely. I make a decision today to refuse to see myself as badly done by. I am blessed and I am grateful.

I rejoice in You! I thank You for Your kindness to me. I celebrate Your goodness to me. I praise You with all of my heart!

In Jesus' name,

Amen

Declarations

Remember, the Word of God is powerful and it changes us. Take these Bible verses and speak them over your life:

"Rejoice in the Lord always. Again I will say, rejoice!" Philippians 4:4

"I will be glad and rejoice in You; I will sing praise to Your name, O Most High." Psalms 9:2

"Enter into His gates with thanksgiving, and into His courts with praise. Be thankful to Him, and bless His name." Psalms 100:4

"Passing through the Valley of Weeping (Baca), they make it a place of springs; the early rain also fills [the pools] with blessings. They go from strength to strength [increasing in victorious power]..." Psalms 84:6-7 (Amplified)

"And let the peace of God rule in your hearts, to which also you were called in one body; and be thankful." Colossians 3:15

Chapter 7
MY EGO

"Listen, I have had another dream," he said.
"The sun, moon, and eleven stars bowed low
before me!" Genesis 37:9

One day as I was worshipping the Lord, I heard Him whisper just one word to me: 'impressed'. In that moment, God conveyed a lifetime of attitudes. With that one word, God convicted me of something rooted deep within that had to change immediately. From early on in my Christian walk, I had a strong sense of the call of God on my life. I received several significant prophecies which confirmed that the Lord wanted to use me. I was hungry for ministry. But wrapped up in that yearning to lead was a desire for prominence. Every word that alluded to fame or success excited me. There was no doubt that my motivation for ministry was to please God and do His will. However, I also loved the thought of the limelight.

When God said 'impressed' to me, I instantly understood what He meant. I was impressed by mighty ministries. I was impressed by jumped-up job titles. I was impressed by important people. I was impressed by big congregations. I was impressed by powerful anointings. I was even impressed by the call of God on my own life. As I fell to my knees, I wept and repented. Romans 12:16 says, "Do not set your mind on high things but associate with the humble". My mind was focused on high things. I needed a system reset. Scripture instructs us not to think of ourselves more highly than we ought, but instead to be sober-minded. I thought that my gifts and call made me a bit more important than other people. How wrong I was.

Being impressed can be dangerous. It can cause us to focus on the wrong things. We should not put people or jobs on pedestals. It is important to honor leaders, but only Jesus deserves adoration. If we treat ministers like stars, we can make it hard for them to walk in humility. Because I saw well-known preachers as celebrities, I thought that if I made it in ministry, I would become a star too. In reality, the word minister means servant and that is my calling. While I was dazzled by God's plans for my life, I was not ready to fulfil them. Once they no longer amazed me and instead just provoked gratitude and love, I was in the right place.

Dazzled by dreams

Joseph grew up knowing he was his father's favorite. The extra attention probably created great confidence. But children need a mother's love too. They need the tenderness and reassurance that mums are best placed to provide. Joseph's plucky demeanor may well have hidden a deep insecurity that took root on the day Rachel died.

When people are raised in a dysfunctional family, it can create a breeding ground for all sorts of heart problems. Insecurity which lurks beneath a veneer of confidence can make us vulnerable to a vast array of issues. One of those is pride. There is not much debate that Joseph suffered from an inflated ego as a young man. He reveled in his dad's devotion and probably began to believe that he really was better than his brothers. If we secretly struggle with insecurity, it is all too easy to draw reassurance from the false notion that we surpass others in some way.

When God showed him his destiny, I think Joseph was enamored by how bright his light would one day shine. He told everyone that he had seen a picture of himself being promoted above his whole family. The dreams may have made him swagger a little. He must have thought to himself: "Wow, I'm going places!" He seems to have been dazzled by his own destiny and he went around telling people about it. Joseph was probably pleased that he was destined for prominence. However, if that was the case, he was focusing on the wrong end of the stick. God does not want us to be fixated by glamour. He wants us to be excited about being a blessing. Prominence is for a purpose. The way Joseph responded to the promise suggested he was probably not yet ready for greatness.

God could not use Joseph while he thought his destiny was about being promoted. After a thirteen year process of transformation, Joseph was prepared to be a servant-leader. He no longer saw fame as glamorous. He saw it as functional. When Pharaoh called him from prison to the palace to interpret his dreams, Joseph could have waxed lyrical about his talents. However, he would not sing his own praises. Instead, when Pharaoh asked him about his gift, he said something like this: "It is not about me; it is God who will turn this situation around". His new heart and changed attitude made him a man that God could use to sustain scores of families through a devastating famine and to save two nations.

Making a good impression

Hezekiah was one of Israel's best kings. He loved the Lord, served Him with all his might and did what was right in His sight. At the same time, he had a weakness. Towards the end of his reign, he received a very special visitor. Remember, Israel was a tiny nation so when the son of the Babylonian king came to visit Hezekiah, he was blown away. The Bible says that he was very attentive to the royal party. Perhaps he was thinking, "Wow, one of the most powerful people in the world has come to see me... I must make a good impression!" When we are impressed, we often want to make a good impression in return. We want people to think well of us. It is not just an Old Testament problem. Why do we name-drop? Perhaps it is because we are enamored when we meet someone special and we think it may dazzle others too.

King Hezekiah decided to show off his nation's vast array of treasures to his highly esteemed guests. Surely they would be amazed that his country had such an exquisite collection of expensive spices, fine gold and silver, precious ointments and armory. After the royal party left, God sent Isaiah to confront Hezekiah about what he had done. As a consequence, every item that the Babylonians had seen would be carried away into captivity, along with the people of Israel. His desire to show off ended up costing Israel everything.

I don't know what you want people to know about you. I used to want acquaintances to understand that I had occupied lots of important positions working for reputable and well-known organizations. Why? I thought it might help to make me look good. Even Paul the apostle was tempted to blow his own trumpet: "Though I might desire to boast, I will not be a fool..." 2 Corinthians 12:6. It feels good to the flesh when we talk about our triumphs. It can make us feel powerful when our stories trigger the admiration and applause of others. Unfortunately, that is not God's way. He loves it when we celebrate the achievements of others instead. He is pleased when we genuinely give all the glory to God. It is a sure way of keeping our ego on a leash.

Brutal truths

One evening, I was having a discussion with my husband. He was upset with me for sending out an email that he thought sounded arrogant. Then he piped up, 'What really bothers me is your self-importance.' I said nothing. Instead, I sat quietly, thinking carefully about what he had said. It was brutal but true. I had started to believe that I was really something and it was changing me for the worse. The Bible warns us about arrogant attitudes in Galatians 6:3: "If anyone thinks himself to be something when he is nothing he deceives himself." Scripture tells us not to think more highly of ourselves than we ought, but to think soberly (Romans 12:3). What's my station? A servant. I was behaving like a jumped-up boss. I eventually thanked my husband for pointing out my error and went to the Lord in prayer. I was brought back to the truth and started to see things as they were once again. As a pastor, my job is to serve my sheep. Without them, I have no ministry.

When Mary the mother of Jesus was told about her history-making destiny, she harbored the prophecy in her heart. She was in awe of God and humbled by His choice. What an example. When we hear about the good things that God wants to do in us and through us, let us remember Mary. When we are picked for promotion or singled out because of our success, let us give God all the honor and thank Him for His favor.

Foundational cracks

Many years ago, I attended a training course on communication styles for Christian leaders. The lecturer outlined what he described as some universal psychological needs. There were six major themes: acceptance, appreciation, respect, recognition, significance and support. He encouraged us to look within and identify which of these we needed for our personal fulfilment.

There were those who felt a deep need to be accepted by the people around them. This made them feel fulfilled. Others longed for appreciation. Whenever they did something admirable, it was important that they were thanked. When no one showed gratitude, it made them feel cheated. Some looked for respect. It gave them a sense of worth and dignity. Respect provided the proof that they were of value. I was split between two: the desire for recognition and significance. I wanted to be celebrated for my achievements. I loved the admiration I received when I succeeded. On the other hand, I yearned to make a real difference in the world. Finally, there were those who needed the support of key people and to have their backup when it really counted.

The problem is that all of these may be the product of foundational cracks in our souls. We can describe these longings as psychological needs or we can allow the light of God's Word to shine in our hearts and reveal what's really going on. Issues on the inside can cause us to veer into what the Bible calls 'the pride of life'. It is interesting to look at different translations of this phrase. The Amplified refers to "assurance from earthy things", the New Living Translation calls it "pride in our achievements" and The Message says "wanting to appear important." I think that sometimes our foundational faults cause us to hanker after the wrong things.

Like many of us, Cain struggled in this area. When he brought a gift to God, the Bible says that the Lord did not respect his offering. He appreciated Abel's sacrifice but not Cain's. Scripture suggests that Cain wanted to be respected and was looking to be honored. To be denied that was too much for his flesh and he lashed out at his brother in anger. God clearly believes that we should be able to handle disrespect from others. I'm sure His plan was to train Cain through life's lessons, yet the young man would not listen.

The truth is that we really don't need to be recognized or respected. The Lord does not want us to derive purpose or fulfilment from people's opinions or reactions. All of those words relate to man's view rather than God's. That is why it is the pride of life. We are called to have the same attitude as Jesus who made Himself of no reputation. To live that way, we must know that our value comes from belonging to the Lord and not from what people think about us.

The superstar within

The Lord often strips away the issues of our hearts in layers. A couple of years after He convicted me of my preoccupation with making an impression, God spoke to me again. I was at a prayer meeting where my husband Paul was ministering from Titus 1:5: "...Set in order the things that are lacking..." Paul asked us to invite the Holy Spirit to reveal any areas in our hearts or lives that needed straightening out.

The moment I closed my eyes to seek the Lord, I heard his voice: "You need to evict the superstar within." The truth pierced my heart. A few days earlier, I had been reading 1 Samuel 16. God told Samuel that He had chosen one of Jesse's sons as the new king to replace Saul. The first to be paraded before the prophet was Jesse's first-born Eliab.

In Jewish culture, being a firstborn is a big deal. Firstborns received their father's blessing: a double portion of their inheritance as well as the kudos of being second in command at home. Eliab would have been the obvious choice. However, when Samuel asked the Lord if Eliab was to be king, God responded: "Do not look at his appearance or at his physical stature, because I have *refused* him. For the Lord does not see as man sees; for man looks at the outward appearance, but the Lord looks at the heart." (1 Samuel 16:7)

Why would God refuse a man?

The Hebrew word for refuse is *maas* and it means to reject, to cast away, to spurn. God clearly considered Eliab as a candidate to be king but loathed what he saw in his heart. Scripture states that God *did not choose* his other siblings. In the Hebrew it says He had *lo* (not) *bāḥar* (chosen) every one of Jessie's older sons, yet He *rejected* Eliab.

We get an insight into this firstborn a few verses later. When David was considering fighting Goliath, Eliab was incensed and retorted: "Why did you come down here? And with whom have you left those few sheep in the wilderness? I know your pride and the insolence of your heart..." (1 Samuel 17:28) David's response was brief: "What have I done this time?"

This exchange is a glimpse into Eliab's heart. He spoke with unkind cruelty about David's occupation and humiliated his little brother in public. David's reply shows that this was typical behavior. Eliab clearly saw himself as superior. He looked down on his brother and belittled his efforts. I believe it was that inflated self-image that caused God to *refuse* Eliab.

So when I heard God tell me to evict the superstar within, I was devastated. At the time, I was travelling a great deal. It was just a few weeks earlier that I had returned from a long trip. I remembered my attitude as I arrived at my home church: "I'm here! The globetrotter has returned!" I felt important and enjoyed the attention.

Now God was telling me that if I wanted to fulfil His plans for my life, I had to evict the superstar within. If I wanted the Lord to use me, I had to deal with that person who felt entitled to privileges. I had to put to death the woman who wanted others to celebrate her success. I wept as I repented and asked God to remind me of my true position: a servant in the house of God.

Ambition

God is creative, merciful, powerful, loving and wise. Put simply, He is great and we are made in His image. He planned and designed us to do amazing works for Him. We are destined for greatness. It is important that we develop a vision of what God wants to do through us and that we hunger after His purposes. This comes from a love for the Lord and a desire to be used by Him for His glory.

The desire to fulfil our destiny is very different from selfish ambition. That is a hankering after achievement or distinction, a yearning for power, honor, fame, or wealth – accompanied by the willingness to strive to get it. We need to be very careful to guard against selfish ambition. If prominence doesn't dazzle us then obscurity won't discourage us.

If you're ambitious, you feel cheated when others get promoted or recognized. In contrast, someone who desires to be used by Him rejoices when brothers get their breakthrough because the motivation is rooted in the kingdom. The Message interpretation of the Bible helps unpack what selfish ambition really is in the following verses: "Don't push your way to the front; don't sweet-talk your way to the top. Put yourself aside, and help others get ahead. Don't be obsessed with getting your own advantage. Forget yourselves long enough to lend a helping hand." Philippians 2:3-4

Our example

Jesus humbled Himself. He made Himself of no reputation so God highly exalted Him. He is our standard and our role model. When we humble ourselves, the Lord will lift us up. Humility is putting aside our dignity or superiority voluntarily and assuming equality with one regarded as inferior. In the Greek language, humility is a word which means to deflate, to let all the air out. When we humble ourselves, we let all the hype and self-promotion out of our heart and see ourselves the way we really are: blessed and loved children of God.

Jesus went through excruciating pain on the cross. He hung there and died for you and I. Our Saviour went down into hell and took the keys of death and hades. Then God raised Him from the dead in the most miraculous way. That was three difficult days. Yet, after all that, when Jesus was reunited with His disciples, He didn't put His feet up and order iced water with lemon. He made a fire and cooked his disciples breakfast. He never stopped seeing Himself as a servant.

The only time that Jesus explicitly told us to learn from Him during His earthly ministry was when He was revealing His humility: "Learn of Me for I am gentle (meek) and humble (lowly) in heart" (Matthew 11:29 - Amplified). He revealed the true heart of leadership when He explained that He came to serve. The Son of God left heaven, gave up His position and reputation to serve, and thereby save, you and I. I try to think of my life this way: just like the donkey who carried Jesus into Jerusalem. I am a much loved nobody who is called to carry Somebody very special.

Prayer

Heavenly Father,

Thank You for your love and patience with me.

I realize that I have sometimes been impressed and motivated by the wrong things. I have hankered after recognition and respect and looked for the admiration of others. I am sincerely sorry.

I apologize for every time that I have been impressed with people when I should have been in awe of You alone. I am sorry for putting positions and people on pedestals when You alone deserve all the glory. I repent for thinking that my gifts or talents make me more important than others.

I humble myself before You today and ask You to help me take captive every high or proud thought. Please help me to learn from Jesus how to be meek and humble of heart.

I give You all the glory for everything that You do in me and through me. I am very grateful that You choose to partner with me to fulfil Your great purposes. I count it an honor and a privilege.

I worship You and I lay my life before You once again.

In Jesus' name,

Amen

Declarations

Remember, the Word of God is powerful and it changes us. Take these Bible verses and speak them over your life:

"Do not set your mind on high things but associate with the humble" Romans 12:16

"Not unto us, not unto us Oh Lord, but to Your name be the glory" Psalm 115:1

"I do not receive honor from men" John 5:41

"Humble yourselves under the mighty hand of God, that He may exalt you in due time." 1 Peter 5:6

Chapter 8
A HEALED HEART
"He kissed all his brothers and wept over them."
Genesis 45:15

When Joseph saw his brothers again for the first time, he did not show even a hint of harshness. His first response when they were reunited was not judgement. He did not display a sense of superiority. He did not revel in their despair. He cried: "But they did not know that Joseph understood them, for he spoke through an interpreter. And he turned himself away and wept." Genesis 42:23-24

With kindness, Joseph revealed himself to his brothers: "Please come near to me." He showed no bitterness towards them, only benevolence. He was tender. His conversation was designed to relieve their guilt and to reassure them. "Do not be grieved or angry with yourselves," he said in Genesis 45:5. He hugged them. He was bursting with brotherly love: "Then he fell on his brother Benjamin's neck and wept, and Benjamin wept on his neck." Genesis 45:14

There is no evidence of even a scrap of resentment. Think about it for a while. Joseph spent 13 years of his life in captivity - first as a slave and then a prisoner. The Bible describes the cruel conditions Joseph endured in jail: "They hurt his feet with fetters, he was laid in irons" (Psalm 105:18). He suffered all this because his brothers hated him. And yet Joseph was full of love for his siblings. He had their best interests at heart.

Even while Joseph was testing his brothers to check that they had really changed, he was also hatching a plan for their prosperity. He earmarked the best land in Egypt for their new home, he identified work for them to do and gave them a new vehicle. They walked to Egypt, but rode back in the the latest model of chariot! He treated them with love and consideration.

How did he do that?

How was it possible for Joseph to be so tender towards the men who tried to ruin his life? There is only one possible explanation. His heart had been completely healed of every hurt. We can forgive someone, but if we are still wounded, we will be careful to keep them at arm's length. It is almost impossible to open our hearts towards people who have betrayed us unless all the pain has been taken away. Yet Joseph was genuinely happy to see his brothers. He hugged them and loved them.

Now here is the thing. We all get wounded on our journey through life. We go through disappointments and difficulties. We may be marginalized or misunderstood. Things can be said that pierce and things may be done that demoralize. But what do we do about it? We normally just dust ourselves down and then carry on the best we can. We may feel deflated, dry or discouraged. We may avoid situations that could cause further hurt. Our hearts may become a little heavy. In short, many of us end up limping through life.

Release valve

God designed us with a powerful release mechanism for anguish and pain. It is called tears. When they are directed correctly, the results are remarkable. Crying alone will not normally bring lasting relief. Many people weep out of frustration or hurt without getting healed. However, when we learn how to pour out our hearts before the face of the Lord, we will be made whole. I have had the privilege of leading countless people across the world to restoration and refreshing. Men and women who have been rejected, belittled, betrayed or bereaved have been made new in the presence of God.

I am convinced that our hero Joseph learned through years of dejection and deep disappointment how to give his anguish to God in prayer. Genesis records seven different occasions when Joseph wept. He cried loudly, with tears streaming down his face. He wept alone, he wept in front of his brothers and as he hugged his father for the first time since their separation. He knew how to be made whole by pouring out his heart.

The devil recognizes the importance of having a healed heart. Satan also knows that expressing our emotions is vital to our inner wellbeing so he tries to deactivate them. I honestly believe that most people don't know how to release their pain. Some think they are fine. Others know they are not. Most folk carry some sort of unresolved sadness.

Weeping is not weakness

Adults often tell their children to dry their eyes and weeping is seen as a sign of weakness. There is a popular myth that *real men don't cry*. This is simply not true. Joseph sobbed in public on several occasions. Not once did he seem ashamed or embarrassed. In fact, he cried freely and frequently, even though he was the second most powerful man in the land. It is not only Joseph who knew how to weep. We have countless biblical examples of mighty men pouring out their hearts, both in private and public.

King David soaked his bed with tears as he recounted every agonizing trial to the Lord in prayer. Jeremiah cried before God and encouraged the people of Israel to do the same. Paul shed tears freely. The Ephesian elders sobbed when they said goodbye to their leader. And our greatest example, Jesus, wept.

The strongest (and probably the largest) member of our church is a weights trainer, ironically known as Junior. He was raised in terrible poverty during the civil war in Sierra Leone. Junior went hungry and had to wear shoes made of wire. He was nearly killed as a teenager on three separate occasions and witnessed atrocities no one should have to see. After escaping to the UK, the Lord gloriously saved and then healed Junior. This husband and father is now one of the biggest softies I know. When the presence of the Lord visits a meeting, he is one of the first to fall to his knees and worship, with tears streaming down his face.

My husband and I love to watch movies together. If a film is about human tragedy or turmoil, it is not uncommon for both of us to sob. In fact, while I weep, I often find myself praying that the Lord will increase my compassion for the crushed. I always ask for a greater anointing to bring healing to the hurting. On those occasions, my tears release a deeper love for those who desperately need God's help.

The key that unlocks the door

Wounds are usually bound up by words. What do I mean? Imagine that our hearts are like houses with twisting corridors leading to different rooms. When something hurtful happens, it is as though a room inside our soul gets blocked with pain. The way to unlock the door to that room is by returning to the memory in the presence of God and saying what we never said. When we tell the Lord exactly what we went through and how much it hurt, we release the sorrow and healing tears can flow. Lamentations 2:19 says, "Pour out your heart like water before the face of the Lord." When we pour out our hearts, we share the most intimate details of our lives with someone we trust.

After our daughter died, I told God how much I missed my little girl and how empty I felt without her. I wept healing tears as I shared my sadness with the Lord. I made a decision that the grief was better out than in. I poured out my pain in God's presence, and bit by bit, I received remarkable relief. My journey to restoration was made up of a mixture of outpourings in prayer and healing encounters.

The power of encounters

About a month after Naomi died, I decided it was time to tidy her toys. As I packed away her favorite playthings, unbearable pain overwhelmed me. I was in agony. Not knowing how to hold myself together, I cried out to God from the depths of my being: "Help!" Almost immediately, I felt a hand reach down from heaven and into my heart. My heavenly Father pulled out my pain. Within a matter of minutes, the agony was over. I sat on my sofa exhausted and yet astonished at God's goodness.

That is just one example of many healing encounters I experienced in the presence of the Lord. Today, I can talk about our first daughter with great love, but no sorrow. Her birthdays and anniversaries come and go without any sadness. My husband and I are completely healed. Depending on the circumstances of your journey though life, you may need repeated healing experiences. Just as we may have to go to the doctor or hospital on several occasions for certain conditions, so we might need repeated visits to our Heavenly Healer.

The overflow

Restoration never stops with us. God did not only mend my heart. He turned my river of pain into a spring of healing. Every time my team and I minister, people are restored. The Holy Spirit shines His light into the depths of people's souls. He reveals hidden hurt and then He heals. God sets people free from inner issues that they did not even know were hampering their lives. They leave our events refreshed, energized and ready to live life to the full. What He did for me, He will do for you.

2 Corinthians 1:4 says that God "...Comforts us in all our tribulation, that we may be able to comfort those who are in any trouble, with the comfort with which we ourselves are comforted by God." Our Heavenly Father longs to heal every hurt that is hindering your life. He seeks to remove every ounce of sadness on the inside. He will then fill you anew with His Spirit and anoint you to bring that same restoration and refreshing to others. It is a kick in the teeth to the devil every time one of God's children is restored. It adds insult to satan's injury when we go a step further and allow ourselves to become a channel of healing for others.

Spiritual heart surgery

Jack had been in ministry for twenty years when he came to Healed for Life. He booked because someone asked him, not because he thought he needed to receive. He had no idea that he was carrying so many burdens and was overwhelmed by the depth of God's work within: "There are no words to describe what happened at Healed for Life. Since my early twenties, although I was serving God, I still felt incomplete. When things went wrong, all I could think about was all the other things that had gone wrong. I constantly sought validation for whatever I did, and it seemed like I could never be satisfied with the compliments.

"The team at Healed for Life prayed for us during the ministry times and I walked away feeling completely free. It was as though I had been through spiritual open-heart surgery. I don't ever remember being this balanced and focused. For the first time in decades, everything is going in the right direction." When Jack returned home, his world changed. His family moved out of the hotel room where they had been staying and into their own home. Work opportunities opened up and he stepped into a brand new ministry. The Bible says in Proverbs 4:23 that our hearts determine the course of our lives. When we allow Him to heal us, we set ourselves up to succeed.

Try a little tenderness

One of the best by-products of healing is that our hearts can become tender. To explain what something is, it can help if we understand what it is not. We will do this by looking at God's people in the wilderness. After a plethora of extraordinary wonders that led to their escape from Egypt, God separated the Red Sea for them to cross on dry land. Never before in the history of the world had people walked through a parted sea. Once in the wilderness, God provided manna for food and manifested His presence in thunder, lightning, smoke and fire.

Despite this array of mighty miracles, when their water ran out the Israelites complained bitterly and questioned God's goodness. They threw His gifts back in His face and launched an attack on their leader. They disregarded the testimonies of yesterday when they faced the trials of today. They were quick to complain, quick to criticize and quick to forget their blessings. God said that they were hard-hearted.

You might be thinking that a hard heart is a good thing. It keeps you free from unnecessary emotionalism and guards you against vulnerability. It protects you from feeling the effects of the normal wear and tear of life. It helps you to stay strong. God has a different take. He says in Matthew 13:14-15 that hardness of heart prevents us from hearing the voice of the Lord, it stops us from seeing what God has in store for us and it hinders our ability to understand. Hardness of heart is yet another trap of the devil to keep us small. For us to be ready for everything God wants to do in us and through us, we need a soft heart.

Sometimes we forgive those who have robbed us, but retain a mild attitude of antagonism towards them. The Hebrew word for hard is *qasa* and it means tough or severe, grieved or sore. So when our heart is hard towards a brother or sister, we have a slightly more severe view of their affairs. We don't make allowances for their mistakes in the same way that we would for others. We can be quick to feel cross and slow to show mercy. We keep ourselves emotionally detached. A soft heart makes someone quick to forgive, quick to love and quick to say sorry. It also makes a person quick to heal.

Hard towards God

I want to look at two ways we can have a hard heart. The first is when we shut down towards God. The Bible's account of the Israelites in the wilderness illustrates this type of hardness. The Lord had done so much for His people but they forgot His faithfulness. As soon as times became tough, they complained to their leaders and criticized God. The whole atmosphere in the nation changed. They were no longer grateful. They were angry and indignant. Psalms 95:8-9 says, "Do not harden your hearts... in the day of trial..." It is when we are in the wilderness that we need to be most careful. This is when we can all too easily become offended at God.

The Greek word for hard-heartedness is *sklērokardia*. It means rigid. We shut the door on the inside and push God out. We may feel justified because our lives are chaotic. Perhaps you feel God has forgotten His promises. Hebrews 3:15 says, "Today, if you will hear His voice, do not harden your hearts." We can choose to be unmoved by the Word of God or we can choose to respond. God is looking for people who will take down the guard and open up in His presence.

Just as complaining makes us cross, thanking makes us soft. In truth, gratitude is not an optional attitude for Christians. It is God's will. 1 Thessalonians 5:18 in the Amplified says: "Thank God in everything, no matter what the circumstances may be, be thankful and give thanks, for this is the will of God for you who are in Christ Jesus..." When we choose to be thankful irrespective of what is going on, it helps to tenderize our hearts towards the Lord.

When I look back over my life, I often wonder why God overlooked my issues for so long. Yes, I loved the Lord. However, the self-importance, pride and preoccupation with the opinions of others were awful. Recently, I understood something of a redeeming feature that kept the favor of the Lord shining down. Somehow, through the pains and pressures of a difficult life, my heart stayed soft towards God.

Tough towards others

The second way that we can be hard is in our attitude to the people around us. Although I have always been pretty pliable towards God, I have sometimes been cold and hard with others. I can think about specific people against whom I have hardened my heart. I might have appeared courteous, but inside I felt callous. I would prickle in their presence and try to keep them at a distance. Communication would feel a little strained and I would try to avoid being too close for too long. This is symptomatic of someone with a hard heart.

When your muscles are tense, it hurts if someone prods you and you pull away promptly. When your muscles are soft, a poke is painless. It is the same way with our hearts. If my heart is hard then I'm more likely to react in irritation when I am let down. I am more likely to be impatient with their weaknesses. When there is softness, I will be gentler and kinder towards those who once wound me up. I will be more like Jesus.

Sometimes we batten down the hatches of our hearts because we have never been healed of our hurts. We build walls to try to protect ourselves from further pain. The trouble is, the barricades we put up keep our pain in just as much as they keep other people out. On occasions, in an attempt to relieve pain, we either block out or distance ourselves from hurt. We stop allowing ourselves to feel the ache and instead close the door. If that's you, please start, or continue on, your journey to wholeness. The more we are healed of every hurt, the easier it is to be kind and tender towards others.

At other times, we can be tough because of intolerance. People around us don't live up to our standards. The beginning of change is when we realize that our hearts are hard. It might be an isolated grudge towards one or two people, or perhaps you realize that you are often harsh. God treats us with tenderness when we deserve harshness. He is love and He longs for us to carry His love to others.

Nurturing love

I am sure that Joseph could have felt justified if he shut down and hardened his heart. Instead, he learned to allow the Lord to heal his heart and he nurtured love for his brothers. Little did he know that his destiny was to save his family - the children of Israel. It would have been almost impossible for him to accomplish God's will if he were still deeply wounded. His healing set him free to fulfil his purpose and it enabled God to use him to save two nations.

The Lord doesn't just cause us to forget the past. He restores our souls. As we tell our Heavenly Father exactly what we have been through and how it hurt us, feelings will well up again and the weeping will probably begin. Remember, it only lasts for a night and joy comes in the morning. The depth of security and stability that comes from His healing love makes returning momentarily to the pain worth it.

As we open up our hearts afresh to our Heavenly Father, He is able to tenderize our souls so that we become a channel for His love and compassion: "I will take out your stony, stubborn heart and give you a tender, responsive heart." Ezekiel 36:26 (New Living Translation). We need to become tender towards God and towards the people around us. Compassion *moved* Jesus because His heart was soft. He responded to the hurts and needs of people's lives because He was full of love.

If there are people that you are often impatient with or harsh towards, God wants to break down the barriers. Perhaps they once hurt you or maybe they often mess up. A soft heart changes our attitudes and behavior towards those we once resented. Softness brings relief from the temptation to go back to anger. It releases mercy and kindness.

Prayer

Heavenly Father

Thank You for caring about every issue in my life. I ask You to search my heart and shine Your light into the depths of my soul. Reveal every inner issue that is holding me back and uncover unhealed hurts deep within so that I may be healed. Where my emotions have been shut down, I ask You to open them up again. I ask You to heal me in any area where I need it so that I can be a channel of love and healing to others also. Lead me on a journey to inner security and peace.

Forgive me for the times that I have shut down my heart to your presence. I am sorry for complaining when I could have been thanking. I choose an attitude of gratitude and ask for your help to become a thankful person.

I thank You that you designed me to have a soft and kind heart towards the people around me. I ask You to break up the fallow ground of my heart. I ask You to take out my heart of stone and instead give me a soft, tender heart.

I am sorry for the times that I have been abrupt, impatient or harsh. I am sorry for the people I have held at a distance in disdain. I ask You to forgive me. I choose to see them through Your eyes of love. I choose to be patient and kind to them.

Pour out Your Spirit into my heart afresh today, I pray.

In Jesus' name,

Amen

Declarations

Remember, the Word of God is powerful and it changes us. Take these Bible verses and speak them over your life:

"Pour out your heart like water before the face of the Lord." Lamentations 2:19

"Blessed be the God and Father of our Lord Jesus Christ, the Father of mercies and God of all comfort, who comforts us in all our tribulation, that we may be able to comfort those who are in any trouble, with the comfort with which we ourselves are comforted by God." 2 Corinthians 1:3-4

"I will take out your stony, stubborn heart and give you a tender, responsive heart." Ezekiel 36:26 (New Living Translation)

"Therefore, as the elect of God, holy and beloved, put on tender mercies, kindness, humility, meekness, long-suffering..." Colossians 3:12

Chapter 9

TALK, TALK

"I was stolen away from the land of the Hebrews"
Genesis 40:15

After more than a decade of dire difficulty, Joseph met two of the king's staff in prison. Before he interpreted their dreams, he explained the circumstances of his incarceration: "I was stolen away from the land of the Hebrews; and also I have done nothing here that they should put me into the dungeon." Genesis 40:15

Joseph had a captive audience. These men desperately needed what he had: an answer. It would have been all too easy for Joseph to take the chance to tell his terrible story. He could have told them all about the betrayal of his brothers and their foul plot to make money out of his misfortune. The stripping, the beating, the betrayal, the abandonment. Yet he accused no one. If he alluded to anyone being to blame for his trials, it was our real enemy satan, otherwise known as *the thief*.

I have no doubt that one reason why Joseph said nothing negative was that his heart was healed. Likewise, with us, once the pain has been taken away, there are no more words to say. When you have poured out your heart in the presence of the Lord, there is no real need for anyone else to know the full circumstances.

Two years later, Joseph was promoted from prison to the palace. Pharaoh must have wondered how a Hebrew man ended up in Egypt. In deciding to appoint him to power, he will surely have asked him about his life. Yet Joseph did not tell Pharaoh or his friends in government anything negative about his family. How can I be so sure? If Pharaoh had heard about the brutal behavior of Joseph's brothers, he would no doubt have treated them with great contempt. Instead, when Pharaoh was told that Joseph's siblings were in town, he was delighted and insisted that they were treated to the best of everything. Joseph protected his destiny (and even the future of his nation) by watching what he said.

The real culprit

I don't know what you have been through or who has caused you hurt or harm. Nonetheless, the Word says that our battle is *not* against flesh and blood. Yes, we all must accept responsibility for our choices, but there is only one who is really to blame for the pain we endure. The devil came to steal, kill and destroy. He is our enemy. He is the thief.

When we have been through trial and turmoil at the hands of a fellow human being, sometimes we long for the day when we can show them that they were wrong. When we are betrayed, we often want the perpetrators to face their failings. We want to rise high in front of those who doubted or belittled us. Somehow that will feel like fairness. If you are anything like me, you will have rehearsed speeches pointing out the errors of those who hurt you. In reality, though, all this does is prolong our process.

After nine years as Pharaoh's number two, Joseph was reunited with his brothers. Imagine being in his situation. Having risen to the top of the tree, this is your chance to make them squirm.

Even if you had forgiven, you might seize the opportunity to remind them of their mistakes and make them suffer for a while.

Not Joseph. God had done such a deep work in his heart that he adopted a very different approach: "I am Joseph your brother, whom you sold into Egypt. But now, do not therefore be grieved or angry with yourselves because you sold me here; for God sent me before you to preserve life." Genesis 45:5. The first thing Joseph said to his brothers was intended to relieve their guilt and set them free from condemnation. He explained that their actions had been turned around for the good and used as part of God's plan for their future deliverance. Joseph had no desire to lord it over them. He was tender and kind.

Joseph's family reunion took place twenty two years after he saw his brothers bow before him in his dreams. His promotion nine years earlier was confirmation that the rest of the picture would come to pass. Joseph did not know when he would see them again, but I think he probably prepared himself. Perhaps at first, he planned to make them pay a little. However, as God worked on his character, Joseph was ready for the momentous reunion. He was ready to be loving.

False accusation

Not long after my husband and I were married, we went through a terrible trial. Our church finances were diminishing quickly because we were tithing to two different organizations. Our ministry was small in size and every penny counted. My husband knew that we would have to reorganize to stop the hemorrhage. He sought advice and consulted his superiors, then made the necessary changes. We both believed everyone involved was in agreement.

To our surprise, at our next church management meeting we were accused of a whole host of impropriety. It was not just what they were saying, but how it was said. Vicious verbal attack after vicious verbal attack left us bewildered and wounded. It did not stop there. Phone calls were made to members of our leadership team claiming that we were in rebellion. Rumors about us spread and people in our wider Christian network who once admired us suddenly kept their distance.

One night, I was in so much turmoil that I was unable to sleep. I was due to preach that Sunday and knew I could not do so in that state. I crept out of bed and went into our office. I poured out my heart before the Lord. I told Him how much their words had hurt, how unfair it all felt. I wept as I explained how much it all wounded me. Soon, my tears dried up and my peace was restored. The ache was gone so I went back to bed.

God is the vindicator

It was not long before these allegations of impropriety and insubordination were brought to the apostolic leaders over us. There were calls for our dismissal. We hadn't done anything wrong, but we were now at risk of losing everything. As my husband sought the Lord, He instructed us to hold our peace. God told us that we should not attempt at any point to vindicate ourselves. He warned us not to say anything negative about anyone involved and He led us to walk in love. I have no doubt that the healing I received from heaven enabled me to keep my peace with people. I was able to constrain myself around others because I had poured out my heart before the Lord. Within three months, God Himself completely vindicated us.

False accusations can be emotionally crippling. We don't like it when we are misunderstood, mainly because most of us want to be liked. There are times of course when we need to set the record straight, but the answer is never retaliation or vengeance. If you can learn to hold your peace and trust God for justice, you will be amazed at what He will do for you. Joseph was falsely accused of rape. To know that you are pure and yet be accused of a brutal attack must have been agonizing. However, Joseph maintained his dignity. He refused to criticize those who had hurt him and instead focused on allowing God to work on him. We must remember that the Lord sees everything: "God is witness" (Genesis 31:50b). It is His opinion that counts and He loves it when we are benevolent towards those who don't deserve it.

What about when we're discouraged?

It is easy to celebrate the faithfulness of God when we are on the mountaintop. When everything around us seems to be falling apart is when we need to hold our tongues. Unfortunately, the children of Israel never seemed to grasp this precept. They would joyfully sing God's praises when the Lord performed mighty miracles. When they were disheartened, they would quickly start to complain and criticize: 'They journeyed... and the soul of the people became very discouraged on the way. And the people spoke against God and against Moses: "Why have you brought us up out of Egypt to die in the wilderness? For there is no food and no water, and our soul loathes this worthless bread."' Numbers 21:4-5

The Hebrew word in this verse for discouraged means cut down, grieved, troubled and vexed. When we are disheartened, it can be very difficult to remember His promises. King David lost everything when he was living in a city called Ziklag. He and his army returned from a thwarted battle to discover that their homes had been burnt to the ground and their wives and children taken captive. On top of that, David's men turned on him, blaming their

93

leader for their loss and pain. It would have been easy for David to complain and even curse God. Instead he exercised self-control and encouraged himself.

Perhaps he reminded himself of the faithfulness of God. Maybe he went back to the prophecy he received from Samuel that one day he would be king. He may have praised God despite his pain. We don't know how he did it, but David spoke words of strength to his own soul and faith arose once again. He used his own faith-filled words of encouragement to pull himself out of a deep, dark hole.

The Israelites were not quite so constrained. They were exhausted and disappointed. Their journey was longer and harder than they had ever expected it to be. Families with small children and elderly relatives walked for miles in searing temperatures and hard conditions. In truth, testing times are our opportunity to find out what we are really made of. That is when we discover how dependable we really are. The Israelites could not handle the delays. They criticized their leaders and blamed God. They allowed every thought going around in their heads to escape out of their mouths!

A long night

A few years ago, in the middle of winter, I travelled to Pittsburgh to assist a friend at a conference. I started to feel ill towards the end of the convention. Soon, I had a fever. I carried on as best I could, but was very glad when it was time to head home. I was taking a flight to New York so I could catch another plane to London. As I waited, fog descended. My eyes were glued to the departures board as the delays clocked up. 30 minutes became an hour. Two hours became a three hour delay. Before I knew it, I had missed my flight to London.

Something inside me said that I must not let anything but thankfulness out of my heart. When I reached New York, I arranged a new flight home for the following morning. But by the time that was sorted, all the comfy seats in the draughty waiting area were gone. I lined up four wooden chairs, put my bag under my head and pulled my coat over myself. As I lay awake all night fighting a fever, all that left my heart was worship. I kept telling God how grateful I was for the privilege of being able to call myself a minister.

When I eventually reached London, I waited at the carousel for my luggage. You guessed it: my bags didn't arrive. I filled out the necessary forms, then headed home - still loving the Lord. About two days later, the bags were dropped off at my house. With a smile, I thanked the delivery driver and then my heavenly Father. At that moment, I sensed the Lord say, "Well done daughter, test passed." I was stunned. But I learned a lifelong lesson that night. The best route through the toughest of times is to avoid complaining at all costs. Do whatever it takes to remain thankful in the midst of the fire. Life is much more enjoyable when we are grateful.

The steering wheel

The Bible says that our tongues are the steering wheels of our lives. They direct our course. Part of growing up spiritually is learning to apply self-control in our conversation. It can be a fierce fight with our carnal nature, but we need to learn to restrain our flesh and bite our lip. When someone has wronged us and we have a captive audience, it can be very tempting to gratify the flesh and say something spiteful. However, it may well be a test we need to pass in order for us to be ready for our destiny.

Next time you feel like describing the errors of a fellow human being, I invite you to stop yourself and deliberately bless them instead. When you want to moan, put your hand to your mouth and instead thank God for something good He has done for you. It demands determination as the urge to criticize or complain can be overwhelming. Yet the more we restrain ourselves, the easier it becomes. Holding your peace will eventually become second nature. The Bible tells us to speak well of those who hurt us: "Bless those who curse you, do good to those who hate you and pray for those who spitefully use you..." Matthew 5:44

This is a principle that Joseph lived by. At some point during his painful process, he must have made some serious decisions. Perhaps he understood that if he showed mercy, he would reap it when he needed it the most. The result? He refused to sow negative ideas about his brothers in the hearts of his hearers. Maybe he knew the power of the tongue. You see, words are seeds. You will have experienced it yourself. Perhaps you trusted someone until a friend told you something suspicious about that person. Their comment planted a seed of doubt. We need to watch that we don't do that ourselves. When we sow seeds of cynicism, we are influencing other people's attitudes and may be curbing their compassion.

We all make mistakes. That's a given. We have a choice about whether we share the errors of others with family and friends. I am not questioning the value of opening up to our closest companions in the pursuit of personal freedom. That is vital. I am suggesting we can learn from Joseph's example and seek to protect and bless even those who have hurt us.

Prayer

Heavenly Father,

Thank You that I can tell You everything. When I pour out my heart before You, it releases trapped pain. When I share my deepest disappointments with You, I will receive Your wonderful healing love. Help me to direct my pain to You and not to people.

I thank You that my mouth has the power to sow seeds in other people's hearts about my brothers and sisters. I ask You to cleanse my tongue and clean my mouth. Help me, Lord, to purify myself by watching what I say. I am sorry for the times when I have criticized others, grumbled or complained. I ask You to forgive me.

I ask You to help me put a guard over my mouth so that only goodness and gratitude come out. Help me to train my tongue so that my words help and not hinder my progress.

I pray that when You hear me talk, it will be a blessing to Your ears.

In Jesus' name I pray,

Amen

Declarations

Remember, the Word of God is powerful and it changes us. Take these Bible verses and speak them over your life:

"Let the words of my mouth and the meditation of my heart be acceptable in Your sight, O Lord, my strength and my Redeemer." Psalms 19:14

"Set a guard, O Lord, over my mouth; keep watch over the door of my lips." Psalms 141:3

"But I say to you, love your enemies, bless those who curse you, do good to those who hate you, and pray for those who spitefully use you and persecute you." Matthew 5:44

Chapter 10

THE POWER OF JUDGEMENT

"Do not be afraid, for am I in the place of God?"
Genesis 50:18b

When God turns your situation around, you may find yourself in a position where you can exercise revenge for the pain or humiliation you endured at the hands of others. For the sake of our own destiny, it is vital that we follow love's way. Thirteen years of slavery and imprisonment gave Joseph every right to seek retribution. It would have been completely justifiable for him to make his brothers pay for their cruelty. Furthermore, the perfect opportunity presented itself. Joseph had it all - position, power, prosperity - and his brothers had nothing. He could have lorded it over them. Yet right from the start of their reunion, Joseph was gracious.

Even after enjoying many years of peace and prosperity in Egypt, the sons of Jacob clearly thought there was a possibility that Joseph had only been good to them since their reunion for the sake of their father. When Jacob died, the brothers were terrified that Joseph would take his chance to exact revenge. In fear for their lives and their families, they hatched a plan. The 11 told Joseph that their dad had instructed them to come after his death to see their brother to ask for forgiveness.

Joseph's response showed the depth of his love for his betrayers. He broke down and wept. However, his words reveal something just as important. What he said shows us one of the keys that helped him keep a soft heart towards the men who tried to destroy his destiny. Joseph said: "Do not be afraid, for am I in the place of God?" Genesis 50:19

God knows

Our hero refused to judge. To Joseph, judgment was God's responsibility. He saw himself as a fellow servant even though he was a lord in the land. He was saying to his siblings, "I don't have the right to judge you and I don't want to anyway." Without even realizing it, he was protecting the purity of his heart. Thousands of years later, Paul the Apostle put it like this: "Who are you to condemn someone else's servants? Their own master will judge whether they stand or fall. And with the Lord's help, they will stand and receive his approval." Romans 14:4 (New Living Translation)

I am not responsible for anyone else's actions. I am accountable for my own behavior. The Bible teaches that each of us will give an account to God of our own words and our own works. We will never have to report to God on how others fared through their ups and downs. If I focus on the failings of others, I am missing the point. God's heart is always for my restoration when I mess up. He has the same longing for those who have hurt me and He had the same desire for Joseph's brothers too. God never enjoys judgement. He loves releasing His mercy. James 4:12 sums it up: "...Who are you to judge another?"

The honest truth is that we really don't know what goes on in the lives of other people. It does not matter how well we are acquainted with someone. Only God knows their hearts. As a result, we are not equipped to assess their attitudes or actions. That's God's job. When someone has hurt me or let me down, my human instinct is to judge. This is the thought which has often helped me to choose mercy: "Until I have lived your life and walked in your shoes, I don't know that I would have behaved any differently."

The day our daughter died, my husband and I drove home from the hospital in a daze. We were travelling slowly in the fast lane of the highway. A car drew up close behind us and the driver became very impatient. He tooted his horn and shook his fist. Alarmed, we quickly pulled over into the slow lane. I learned an important lesson that day. You never know what is going on in someone else's life. You never know what is causing their behavior.

Revolving door

The Bible says that when we judge others, we open the door to being judged ourselves: "Do not judge or you too will be judged. For in the same way you judge others, you will be judged and with the measure you use, it will be measured to you." Matthew 7:1-2. There are not many occasions in Scripture when God says that if we withhold something, He will too. For example, the Bible says that when we are faithless, He remains faithful. However, there is something about setting ourselves up as a critic of a fellow human being that repels the Lord. If we judge, we will inevitably be judged in return.

I depend on the marvelous mercy of God. I need His mercy to cover my many mistakes and His favor to shine on me despite my shortcomings. I covet the generosity of heart and goodwill of my family and friends. When I fail or slip up (as I often do), I seek their understanding and forgiveness. I need my husband to let me

101

off when I get a parking fine. I want my children to show mercy when I'm short-tempered. I look to my team to be gracious when I get things wrong.

To receive mercy, I need to show mercy to other people. Mercy is about being kind to those who don't deserve it. It is showing love when I want to hate. Romans 14:13 in the New Living Translation says, "Let's stop condemning each other..." Why? Not only do we hold back the graciousness of God when we point the finger, but we are also in danger of getting into further bondage. We risk falling into the very sin that we are criticizing. Romans 2:1 says: "...For in whatever you judge another you condemn yourself; for you who judge practice the same things." Even Jesus said in John 8:15 that He judges no one. If my perfect Savior - who never made a mistake - will not judge, then neither should I.

A heart of humility

To his brothers, Joseph may have sounded proud as a young man. Years later, we can see the transformed heart that testing times had produced in him. Genesis 41:16 records his first conversation with Pharaoh: "'I have heard it said of you that you can understand a dream to interpret it.' So Joseph answered Pharaoh, saying, 'It is not in me; God will give Pharaoh an answer of peace.'"

Joseph refused to draw attention to himself. He said, "It's not my gifting. It's not my talent. It's all God." His heart of humility was the breeding ground for the mercy that he showed. He deliberately chose to see himself as a servant. It is not a servant's place to judge. That is the role of one who is superior. When we have a humble heart, it is much easier to climb down from judgement and instead show people the same graciousness that we have received from God.

To be genuinely humble, we need to know that we are valuable. You and I are precious because we belong to Jesus. You can be perfectly secure in God. That comes when you are convinced of your worth to your Heavenly Father and when you know how much He values you. It is out of that knowledge that we are joint heirs with Jesus that we can put aside our superiority to serve those that we may previously have regarded as inferior. When I really understand that I am a son of God, I can lay aside every privilege and be a servant to His people.

Do you have a "Type A" personality?

How we live our everyday lives is of utmost importance to the Lord. I never really thought of myself as a judgmental person. When it came to the big issues, I could show mercy and compassion. If a friend fell flat on her face, I would want to help her back up again, knowing it could easily have been me. In contrast, if someone made silly mistakes, it would really wind me up. In truth, I did not believe that this was a problem. You see, I liked competence and thought that having high expectations of myself *and* of the people around me was essential.

It has been suggested that people have either a type A or a type B personality. They say type A people are ambitious, highly organized, truthful, impatient and always trying to help others. They take on more than they can handle, want others to get to the point, are proactive and obsessed with time management. They are often high achievers who multitask. They push themselves with deadlines and dislike both delays and ambivalence.

Although I could not identify with all of that description of a type A personality, I could see enough of myself in that picture to make me believe it was me. As a result, expressing intolerance or frustration was part of my psychology and therefore acceptable. Being abrupt or harsh from time to time, although undesirable, was understandable. I had my perfect excuse.

Then God started to speak to me. He put a yearning in my heart to be tender. It's easy to be tough, but God is also tender. I studied Scripture and learned two life-changing lessons. Firstly, tenderness is something we do. And by the way, the 'we' I am referring to are those who are chosen by God and who He calls as sons and daughters. Colossians 3:12 says, "Therefore, as the elect of God, holy and beloved, put on tender mercies, kindness, humility, meekness..." This is not just addressed to Type B people, who are more relaxed and patient by nature, but to all who follow Jesus. Tenderness is something we put on. It is a choice, not a feeling.

Job's so-called friends

Have you ever wondered what lesson we are supposed to learn from Job's friends in the Bible? About thirty chapters are dedicated to their discourses. If you have read the story of Job, you will know that a great deal of what they said was doctrinally correct. I don't believe it was just what they said that caused God to be angry with them. It was the state of their hearts. Job was grief-stricken following the sudden death of his children. His marriage was a mess. His wife had turned her back on God. He was in terrible physical pain. Job did not need doctrine. He did not need his friends to point out his flaws and failings. He needed their love and mercy.

In utter despair, Job sums up how he feels about his so-called friends: "What miserable comforters you are... I could say the same things if you were in my place. I could spout off criticism and shake my head at you. But if it were me, I would encourage you. I would try to take away your grief." Job 16:2,4-5 (New Living Translation)

When we judge people who are in pain, we can do great harm. I know all too well when I have messed up that I don't really need people to remind me. Once again, we see Job talking about the agony of being accused in his time of need: "How long will you torment my soul and break me in pieces with words?" Job 19:2. The Bible says that love covers over weaknesses and faults. We have an opportunity to exercise this love when people around us have made mistakes. We can be an expression of mercy in their lives. According to Romans 2:4, it is the goodness of God that leads to repentance, not our rantings. We can help people towards restoration simply by being gracious.

Put it on

Like I said, there are two lessons I have learned about mercy. The first is that it is something we do.

There are people who need to experience mercy through us. The Lord is longing for us to show His mercy to people who expect to be judged. Just as the Bible teaches us to put on love, it also admonishes us to wear mercy. We can clothe ourselves in His love and treat people exactly the way we would want to be treated if we were in their shoes. Colossians 3:12 says, "Therefore, as the elect of God, holy and beloved, put on tender mercies, kindness, humility, meekness, longsuffering..." The Lord wants us to carry these qualities wherever we go. He wants us to demonstrate His characteristics.

Secondly, it works with tenderness. Mercy and tenderness are a team. As I meditated on a verse that talked about my need to display the tender mercies of God, the penny dropped... If mercy works with tenderness, then judgement works with harshness. It made complete, convicting sense. When I am stroppy, I am reacting to a judgement I have made. For example, if someone is fifteen minutes late for a meeting and I am annoyed, I am taking on the role of their examiner. I'm questioning their competence or professionalism. My assessment of them makes me think that I have the right to be upset: they are below the standard which is required. In contrast, mercy considers their needs and their feelings first.

I decided that I didn't want to judge anyone anymore. I asked God to change my nature. I want to be like Jesus: rich in mercy and believing the best. When I am tender, it is a sign that mercy is flowing. When I am harsh, it suggests judgement is rearing its ugly head again. I am not there yet, but I am definitely a work in progress! My husband says a big Amen to that!

The way to grace

It's all too easy to fall into bad habits. Whether it is commenting on the quality of another person's driving or reacting to assistants at the supermarket, God does not want us to judge others: "If you call someone an idiot, you are in danger of being brought before the court. And if you curse someone, you are in danger of the fires of hell." Matthew 5:22 (New Living Translation)

Jesus was saying that the moment we judge someone else's behavior, we invite judgement upon ourselves. Judgement is the way to leave the realm of grace. Mercy is the method of entry. Both are doors. One leads us into favor and mercy. The other leads us out to a place where we get what we deserve. I would like to tell you something that has really helped me in all this.

I try to remind myself that the very people that I am struggling with are also God's children. Saved or not, they are His creation and He loves them. I want to be careful about talking or thinking negatively about someone He loves just as much as He loves me.

When my son is telling my daughter about her flaws and faults, I will ask him, "Are you her mum? If the day comes when you are her boss, then feel free to point out her failings. Until then, please build her up." In the same way, God is the head of this big family, not me. Just as I love my son and daughter equally, so the Lord cares for each of His people equally.

A better way

Mercy feels good. Sometimes it's hard to get going, but once you're in the flow, it's liberating. It helps to remove strife and tension from your heart and makes room for more patience and understanding. Best of all, the more mercy we show, the more of it we will receive both from God and people: "Blessed are the merciful for they shall obtain mercy." (Matthew 5:7). Blessed means happy, so the happiest people on earth are those who allow graciousness and kindness to flow from within towards those who do not deserve it.

Joseph would not have been ready for his dreams to be fulfilled if he had not allowed mercy to grow on the inside. His destiny was to show mercy to the brothers who betrayed him. We serve a wonderful God who is rich in mercy. His mercy will never wear out. It is who He is and what He does. The Bible says His mercy endures forever. Perhaps He is waiting for you and I to become more like Him, to step down from judgement and begin a journey of learning how to show mercy to people (like us) who don't deserve it.

Prayer

Heavenly Father,

I thank You that Your mercies are new every morning. You overlook my errors and show me favor when I don't deserve it and I am very grateful.

I am sorry for the times when I have judged others for the mistakes that they have made. I apologize for the occasions when I have been harsh and intolerant. I am sorry, Lord, and I ask You to forgive me and I ask You to change my heart and my habits.

According to Your Word, goodness and mercy follow me and I would like these attributes to flow through me to others. I want to become a mercy shower. Help me to be kind to people who do not deserve it. Help me to overlook people's mistakes because You overlook mine.

I have no right to judge people because I am not You, God. You are the only rightful judge. I step down from that high place of examining others and instead choose to be patient, tender and kind.

Help me to become more and more like Your Son.

In Jesus' name I pray,

Amen.

Declarations

The Word of God is powerful and it changes us. Take these Bible verses and speak them over your life:

> *"Blessed are the merciful for they shall obtain mercy."* Matthew 5:7

> *"Therefore, as the elect of God, holy and beloved, <u>put on</u> tender mercies, kindness, humility, meekness, long-suffering; bearing with one another, and forgiving one another, if anyone has a complaint against another; even as Christ forgave you, so you also must do." Colossians 3:12-13*

> *"Do not judge and criticize and condemn others, so that you may not be judged and criticized and condemned yourselves. For just as you judge and criticize and condemn others, you will be judged and criticized and condemned, and in accordance with the measure you [use to] deal out to others, it will be dealt out again to you." Matthew 7:1-2 (Amplified)*

Chapter 11

THE CRUX

"It was not you who sent me here, but God..."
Genesis 45:8

Angela was a bright, articulate woman. After 37 years of marriage, she went through a devastating divorce. Her husband had been abusive, unfaithful and withheld money from her. She felt humiliated, heartbroken and was on the verge of a breakdown. Angela's agony turned to bitterness and hate.

Pastors, friends and family tried to persuade her, but she found it impossible to forgive. She wanted revenge and longed for something terrible to happen to him. Angela was given a copy of my book, 'Lifting the Mask'. Hope grew in her heart. When she read how God healed me, she began to believe that He could restore her too. Angela allowed the love of the Lord to flood into her heart and wash away anguish and pain. She realized that unforgiveness was hurting her more than him. She made a difficult, but firm decision. Angela forgave her husband from the depths of her heart. It took time, yet she relinquished her right to retaliation and gave up her desire for his demise. Making every effort to let go, she released that man into God's hands.

For the first time in many years, Angela experienced real peace and genuine joy. Some months later, she bumped into her ex-husband at a family function. Walking towards him, she reached out her hand and greeted him warmly. The look of shock on his face was a picture. Angela was happy and free.

Joseph's choice

Joseph had every reason under heaven to hold hatred or just plain old anger in his heart towards his brothers. It was not his fault that his father favored him. He did not ask for dreams of greatness. His siblings tried to destroy his destiny because they were jealous. He was just a teenager when they turned on him. As a consequence of their cruelty, 13 years of Joseph's life were seemingly flushed down the drain. For many of us, our twenties are our most adventurous years and they are spent in education or training, exploring our future options. Joseph passed them in captivity.

When his dreams came to pass and his brothers bowed before him, Joseph could have taken vengeance. He chose a different road instead - one that led him to his destiny. He forgave the men who messed up his life. There is not a moment in the account of his reunion when we see anything other than love and mercy. His words sought to reassure them. His hugs conveyed his affection. His generosity displayed his desire for their well-being. These were the actions of a forgiver.

A monumental decision

Our first child became sick before her second birthday. She was rushed to hospital in an ambulance and was admitted to a pediatric ward. Naomi was normally such a chirpy child. She was now limp and lifeless. She needed help. Regrettably, the doctor on duty was determined to get a urine sample before giving my little girl antibiotics. She had not drunk a drop of liquid that day so this was proving terribly problematic. Crucial hours went by.

111

Desperate for the medics to give her something to stop the spread of what we now know was a bacterial infection, I pressed down on my daughter's tiny tummy until I squeezed out a drop of urine into a bowl. I then called to the doctors to give her the antibiotics she so urgently needed. It was too late. The aggressive infection had spread through her bloodstream and eventually caused multiple organ failure. A simple injection of an antibiotic on admission to hospital would have saved her life. It didn't happen and our baby girl died. It felt as though our world had collapsed around us. At that time, Naomi was our only child and she was our joy. Medical reports and subsequent reviews confirmed that the hospital was negligent. Steps were taken to ensure this could not happen again.

As we began to pick up the pieces of our lives, my husband and I made a monumental decision. With tears streaming down our cheeks, we knelt down together in prayer and forgave the doctor who neglected to give Naomi the drugs that would have saved her. Every time that doctor came to mind, we prayed that God would bless her and give her great wisdom. It was like laying aside a heavy boulder. With the anger of injustice laid aside, we could focus our energy on receiving our restoration. I believe that forgiveness helped clear the way for our healed hearts today.

I do not know who has done what to you. However, I do know that holding anger hurts you more than anyone else. The Bible says that resentment destroys (Job 5:2) and that bitterness poisons (Acts 8:23). It seeks a home deep in our hearts and then festers there. It infects our attitudes and robs our joy. Thoughts of indignation crowd our minds and the very people we wish to forget become the focus of our attention. Unforgiveness can drain our energy and corrupt our motives.

But how do I forgive?

Practice makes perfect. Like nearly everything else, forgiveness gets easier the more we do it. Life is full of opportunities to practice. If you are married, you have your greatest trainer right in front of you. Then think about housemates, family, pastors, leaders, teachers, boyfriends, girlfriends and all your friends! Everyone around you will probably do something to irritate, hurt or harm you at some time. Make forgiveness a lifestyle. Even now, think about someone who has done something against you. Choose to let it go and to let them go. Tell the Lord that you don't want Him to hold it against them because you don't hold it against them either anymore.

There are two New Testament words for forgive. The first means give up. So when we forgive someone, it is like giving up a bad habit. All too often, we crave the very substance or lifestyle we are giving up. For example, when we stop eating chocolate or sweets for a season, we crave the taste on our lips. It is the same way with forgiveness. The devil makes sure that it satisfies the flesh when we hold a grudge. However, just as the benefits of kicking a bad habit far outweigh the pain of giving up, so letting go of the wrong someone has done to you gives you fantastic freedom in the end.

The second word for forgive means grace. We all know how we got saved: "By grace through faith." God showed you and I unmerited favor while we were still sinners and died to wipe away our wrongdoing. He did not just forget our sin, He paid the price for our every failing. When we forgive, we show the same graciousness to others that He showed to us. We give to others what we were given by Jesus. We do not do it because they deserve it, but because we want to be like our Lord and Savior:

"And be kind to one another, tender-hearted, forgiving one another, even as God in Christ forgave you." Ephesians 4:32

It's a trap

We also forgive because unforgiveness is a satanic trap. The devil loves it when he can bind us in bitterness because he knows that it gives him legitimate access to our lives. It opens us up to his wicked ways. The devil knows the Word and uses it against us. When he sees us sinning, he takes the chance to oppress us in some area of life. Unforgiveness gives him a foothold. Paul the Apostle considered that holding anger was a risk too great to take: "I have forgiven that one... lest satan should take advantage of us for we are not ignorant of his devices." 2 Corinthians 2:10-11

Although letting go can be hard, it is to our advantage every time. Unforgiveness always does most damage to the one holding it. It can cause hardness of heart, sickness and separation from God. Ironically, it also keeps us connected to the people and pain of the past. When we hold onto anger, we are inadvertently holding on to the person who wronged us. When we let go of the sense of outrage or injustice, we find ourselves letting go of them. The lightness and freedom of forgiveness is phenomenal.

Fiery trials

Many years ago, my husband and I went through a fiery trial. Some leaders levelled fierce accusations at us and a number of core families left our church. It was an incredibly painful period and very nearly destroyed our ministry. I felt so ashamed and dishonored that I told my husband it was like being frog-marched onto the platform at our church and stripped in front of our entire congregation.

DOORWAY TO YOUR DESTINY

After the storm settled and the church ship was stabilized, we had some heart choices to make. Would we wish our former co-laborers the very best, or secretly hope that they would come a cropper? If we want the worst for someone who hurt us, we will ask questions about their lives and hope to hear that times are tough. We will be quick to criticize. We may find ourselves talking about their wrongs freely and frequently, with a sense of superiority.

We had to let go of every ounce of anger. We had to lay down the right to justice. Then we had to choose to love them and wish them well. I said in chapter 1 that we are trained in the university of adversity. Forgiveness is a test that we have to pass in both good and bad times. God always gives us opportunities to graduate with honors and He creates circumstances that will allow us the chance to love against the odds, to go above and beyond the call of duty.

A year or so after everything blew over, we met our former friends. With open arms we hugged and embraced them and rejoiced together as we heard how God had blessed them. I was deeply grateful to God that there was no trace of hurt or resentment left in my heart. I felt very happy.

Don't stop there...

When Joseph's brothers eventually moved to Egypt, Joseph gave them the best place to live: "Joseph situated his father and his brothers and gave them a possession in the land of Egypt, in the *best* of the land." (Genesis 47:11). There was not a bitter cell left in his body because he understood his purpose: to restore those who once rejected him. Joseph practiced a powerful principle thousands of years before Jesus taught His disciples to: "Pray for the happiness of those who curse you, implore God's blessing upon those who abuse you [who revile, reproach, disparage, and high-handedly misuse you]" (Luke 6:28 - Amplified)

Forgiving can be hard. It is sometimes easier to go all out and pray that God will richly bless those who have hurt you. "But I say to you, love your enemies, bless those who curse you, do good to those who hate you, and pray for those who spitefully use you and persecute you..." Matthew 5:44. Going the extra mile and blessing those who have hurt you can help to rid you of all resentment and clear out any remaining bitterness. It cleanses and purifies the soul, making the way for God's blessings to be poured back into your life.

Barbara is a mother of two teenage girls. She had a devastating marriage. It was not just that she had provided virtually every dollar that the family ever lived on. Neither was it that her husband had racked up a secret debt of more than $100,000. He also became a threat to her life. The day came when she had to get out. After the separation, although she was relieved, things seemed to go from bad to worse. He hooked up with another woman and together they started to hurl fierce, false accusations at Barbara. She was broken and bitter and could see no way out. The strain was affecting her health and her doctor was concerned for her well-being.

She had tried forgiveness, but nothing in her heart seemed to change. That was until she started to bless the very people that satan was using to try to destroy her. She treated her blessing sessions like medicine: to be administered three times daily. Barbara persistently prayed for her ex-husband's health, happiness and for his new woman's well-being. In the space of a week, the transformation was visible. Barbara's blood pressure went back to normal, her stress levels reduced and her joy returned. The devil's plan to poison this precious woman was thwarted, once and for all. Now her greatest testimony is the joy she has since completely letting go of every ounce of anger.

Forgiveness and trust

Forgiveness is a free gift that we give to those who have hurt or hindered us. People don't have to deserve it. More often than not, it will feel as though they don't! Trust, by contrast, is earned. One problem some people struggle with is that they don't always understand the difference. I am compelled by love and my longing for freedom to forgive time after time. Trust, on the other hand, involves wisdom and choice. A woman whose husband has repeatedly cheated on her must forgive if she is ever to be free. She may not be able to trust him, though.

When Joseph was reunited with his brothers, he had obviously already forgiven them. His heart was soft towards them and he longed to share his life with them once again. However, he did not yet trust them. Joseph went to great lengths to test his brothers before allowing them back into his life. He devised an elaborate plan, even framing his younger brother for theft, to reveal the true state of their hearts. Once he could see that they had become both honest and honorable, he was ready to open his heart and life to them once again. The Bible says in 1 Corinthians 13 that "Love believes the best". That does not mean that love is foolish or blind. Ask God to give you wisdom if you are in a situation where you are experiencing relentless brutality. He will lead you by His Spirit.

There is a freedom that forgivers enjoy on a daily basis. Resentment and bitterness sap strength, whereas forgiveness and mercy energize. The more we walk in love, the greater the joy we will experience.

Prayer

Heavenly Father,

I am forever grateful that You have forgiven me for every mistake that I have ever confessed to You. When I asked, You wiped away all my sins and made me like new. Your mercies are new every morning and I depend on them. Thank You, Lord.

*I ask for Your help today. I do not want to hold unforgiveness in my heart against anyone. So I come to You and bring **(Name the person or people you need to forgive)** before You. I forgive **(Name)** for everything they have done to hurt or harm me **(Now tell God exactly what you forgive them for doing. For betrayal, rejection, unkindness, etc.)** I let go of what they have done to me. I forgive them. I lay it all down before You and I will not take it up again. And I ask You to forgive them, too.*

*Now I pray for **(Name if they are still alive*)**, I ask You to bless their health, their family, their prosperity. I pray that You will have Your way in their lives.*

I give You all the honor and glory.

In Jesus' name,

Amen

Even if you have to pray this way, like Barbara did, three times a day until you are truly free, it is worth it!

---

* If the person you are forgiving has passed away, you should not pray for them. Forgiving them and letting go of every ounce of angst is all that is required.

Declarations

The Word of God is powerful and it changes us. Take these Bible verses and speak them over your life:

> *"I have forgiven that one... lest Satan should take advantage of us for we are not ignorant of his devices." 2 Corinthians 2:10-11*

> *"Pray for the happiness of those who curse you, implore God's blessing upon those who abuse you [who revile, reproach, disparage, and high-handedly misuse you]" Luke 6:28*

> *"And whenever you stand praying, if you have anything against anyone, forgive him, that your Father in heaven may also forgive you your trespasses. But if you do not forgive, neither will your Father in heaven forgive your trespasses." Mark 11:25-26*

Chapter 12

BECOMING A PILLAR

"Can we find such a one as this, a man in whom is the Spirit of God?"

Genesis 41:381

By the time of his promotion, God had done a deep work in Joseph. The feisty teenager had been transformed into a wise young man that God could use. The Lord had a demanding mission for Joseph so He needed someone who would not fold under pressure. God worked on his chosen vessel through many years of hardship. Consequently, when the nation needed a leader, Joseph was ready. He was mature, strong and full of God's Spirit.

"For our present troubles... produce for us a glory that vastly outweighs them and will last forever!" 2 Corinthians 4:17. This verse says that our difficulties prepare us to shine with His glory. Troubling times transformed Joseph and they can change us too. Here are some of the best results of suffering. I am sure that as you reflect, you will be able to see what God has already done in you. And He who has begun a good work in you will continue until you are fully prepared for His purposes.

1. Resilience and strength

To achieve almost anything in life demands determination. We must be capable of continuing when others give up. We must be able to withstand pressure without caving in. We must be willing to take risks, able to handle failure and ready to obey - no matter what the cost. Put simply, we need to be strong.

We don't build our muscles by reading books about weightlifting. We increase our power by applying hefty pressure in the gym. In the same way, enduring through tough times builds inner strength. When we feel weak, we can become strong simply by carrying on. Being consistent when you feel like giving up creates tenacity. Continuing through thick and thin makes you resilient. Keeping our promises even when it hurts builds integrity.

During the first year of our marriage, God was teaching me to always do what I said I would do. Keeping your word is one of the vital tenets of Christian strength. Our apartment was in need of a clean. As I left for work, I told my husband that I would vacuum the carpets when I got home. That night I cooked dinner, my husband and I ate and we relaxed. Then, as I was getting ready for bed, I remembered my words. It was 11 o'clock at night. I was tired and I had to be up early. Nonetheless, something inside told me that it was time to learn integrity. Even though it was late and I was exhausted, I kept my promise. That was my first step on the road to dependability.

Carrying weight

A large church in Bogota, Colombia, was growing so rapidly that it needed a bigger building and fast. An exciting new sanctuary that could cater for colossal crowds was erected and a dedication service was planned. The evening before the grand opening, a section of the auditorium unexpectedly collapsed. Thank God, this accident happened during the night and not the following day when the building would have been full to capacity. Upon inspection, it became clear that one of the pillars was not strong enough to hold up the massive structure. It had not been reinforced, nor had it been tested. The pillar had collapsed and taken the entire back section down with it.

The kingdom of God needs pillars: people who can carry the weight of responsibility in church and in the community. It needs steely strong people who are immovable and dependable. Possibly the best way that you and I can grow in strength is by learning to endure pressure and pain. When you embrace seasons of difficulty as opportunities to grow, you come out the other side with greater stature and stability. You can then look back and be thankful for the transformation.

Carrying on

I will never forget the message a friend of ours preached at our church after our two-year-old daughter died. Everyone was affected by the loss. Our people were struggling to understand why their pastors had been robbed so terribly. Grief was hovering and people needed help if not answers. Our friend preached the kind of message only a pastor could minister. He exhorted us to continue doing the things we knew how to do. There is something about carrying on which makes you and I strong. The temptation in the midst of trauma is to give up, to stop praying, to push the Bible to one side and quit fellowship. That is exactly what the enemy wants for every one of us. To endure is to carry on regardless. I was broken-hearted in that season, yet I probably seemed strong. Why? I simply stuck to God's plan for my life.

The truth is that promotion brings new battles. We need to become strong where we are now so that we can endure where we are going: "If you have run with the footmen, and they have wearied you, Then how can you contend with horses? And if in the land of peace, in which you trusted, they wearied you, then how will you do in the floodplain of the Jordan?" (Jeremiah 12:5). Successful companies across the world are introducing new recruitment policies. They will not hire people who have not known what it is to fail. Instead, they look for those who have fallen and have demonstrated the strength to get up again. If you look back to the time before your latest trial, I think you will see growth that could not have happened any other way. Every day that you endure, you are getting stronger.

The effects of fighting

Throughout biblical history, God used war to train His people. In fact, the Lord left enemies around Israel to teach them to fight: "Now these are the nations which The Lord left... So that the children of Israel might be taught to know war..." Judges 3:1-2. Sometimes we relish the battle when we are in a good place and full of faith. However, it was fighting during terrible trials that developed David into a man of steel. He loved King Saul as a son loves his father and yet he was forced to contend with the man who he once called his mentor. The process was harrowing, but through it David grew: "Now there was a long war between the house of Saul and the house of David. But David grew stronger and stronger…" 2 Samuel 3:1

David lived the life of a fugitive. Every day of difficulty was preparing him for his calling. The pain of war developed David for leadership. No matter how tough it gets, remember that God is able to turn your circumstances around at the flick of a switch. And at the right time, He will. When and how He fulfils His promises is His business. How we respond to life's battles is our business. The better we get at enduring with dignity, the sooner we will become the person who can possess our promise. Years of struggles strengthened David until eventually he was ready to become Israel's greatest king. In the same way, the Bible says of the Israelites: "The more they afflicted them, the more they multiplied and grew." (Exodus 1:12). Every trial you have endured is strengthening you and increasing your capacity to carry God's blessings.

2. Maturity and character

Suffering has the power to develop depth and maturity in you and me. God is looking for people who are ready for responsibility. Testing times can develop our character and prepare us for prominence: "Consider it pure joy, my brothers and sisters, whenever you face trials of many kinds, because you know that the testing of your faith produces perseverance. Let perseverance finish its work so that you may be mature and complete, not lacking anything." James 1:2-4 (New International Version)

Mature people are strong and stable. They respond when others react. They stand back and wait for an answer while others anxiously bang down doors. It is reassuring being around mature men and women. They are not unsettled by storms because they have seen it all before. They have been perfected by adversity: "We glory in tribulations, knowing that tribulation produces perseverance and perseverance, character; and character, hope." Romans 5:3-4

Tribulation is an old-fashioned word for trouble or pressure. Hard times teach us how to persevere, and the process of enduring builds character within. God's house is not made of bricks and mortar. He builds His temple with people. Pillars in God's kingdom must not only be strong enough to carry the weight of responsibility. They must have the character to withstand temptation and trial. God is looking for people who are robust enough to withstand intense pressure without cracking.

Growing up

When the Lord was looking for someone to minister to the church at Philippi, He chose Timothy. He did not select him because of his gifting, but because of his character: "But you know his proven character, that as a son with his father he served with me in the gospel, therefore I hope to send him at once." Philippians 2:22-23. We don't develop character in the limelight. We build it by serving. We don't become steadfast by watching our dreams come true. It comes when we are consistent even though we are disappointed. You might be wondering what's been going on. You may have received promises and prophecies of breakthrough. However, it seems as though nothing is happening. You think you are exactly where you were a year ago and you can't possibly see the way ahead. God sees the same situation differently. If you have been developing your character in those times, then it will show through.

There are times when I have waited for my children to be ready for a blessing. My daughter was desperate to travel home from school with her friends. She kept asking and pleading. I watched and waited. I observed her crossing roads, interacting with adults and handling money. While she thought I was ignoring her wishes, I was tracking her maturity. Then one day, apparently out of the blue, I told her that she was free to use public transport. Often we think nothing is happening. It feels like our Heavenly Father has forgotten. All the time He is watching and waiting for us to be ready. Then He releases His blessing.

He makes a way

God is at work. Sometimes when we are driving, we come across roadworks. They are usually flanked by signs that say: 'Expect delays' or 'Follow Diversion'. They are annoying, but we get to our destination in the end. I don't know what bumps you have encountered on the road or what hold-ups you have faced. However, I do know that you serve the world's best navigator, who will make a way where there was no way. And while He is re-routing your journey, He is working on your heart. Romans 5:4 in the Amplified version of the Bible says: "Endurance develops maturity of character." To mature, we must endure. We will never learn to endure if there is nothing difficult happening. When times are tough, you are learning to persevere despite the pain.

Paul told Timothy to: "Endure hardship as a good soldier of Jesus Christ" (2 Timothy 2:3). I think if Paul were around today, he might have said it like this: "Suck it up, soldier!" Paul knew that pain and hardship were part of the Christian package. The apostle told his spiritual son to stop feeling sorry for himself and to take it on the chin. The more we endure, the more we mature: "It is good for me that I have been afflicted, *that I may learn.*" (Psalm 119:71). The psalmist acknowledged that, far from being damaging, difficulty was to his advantage because he learned and grew. I'm not talking about self-induced trials or sickness. Rather, the painful tests we go through on our way to success. "Blessed is the man who endures temptation; for when he has been approved, he will receive the crown of life which the Lord has promised to those who love Him." James 1:12

With you all the way

God is for you. He created you and chose you for His purposes. He is more committed to your success than you are. Like a parent helping their child through school, the Lord has set up training courses - otherwise known as pressure and hardship – for you and I. He then stays with us the whole way through. That's the loving Father that we serve. A great leader once said,

"If you want to fulfil a small purpose, God will honor that. However, if you want God to do something great through you, He will dig deep in your character."

A friend of mine put it like this: "Don't waste your pain." It is nearly always part of the process. When you continue serving and remain dependable even when everything inside wants to throw in the towel, that's maturity. When you love the Lord even though friends and family have forsaken you, that's character. The cost is colossal, but it's worth everything. "For you have *need* of endurance so that after you have done the will of God, you may receive the promise". Hebrews 10:36

We need perseverance to fulfil our potential. We need to hold on in order to break through. The promise is our reward for enduring through thick and thin. Even Jesus endured angst and agony for the sake of the joy ahead of Him. Let your reward motivate you to persevere! "Consider Him who endured such hostility from sinners against Himself, lest you become weary and discouraged in your souls" Hebrews 12:3.

3. Loyalty

The birth of our youngest child was traumatic. As the baby's head emerged, medics realized that the umbilical cord was wrapped twice around her neck. Every push was strangling my little one. She was born grey and lifeless, having been starved of oxygen for ten minutes. The baby was rushed by doctors to intensive care and I lay there wondering if I'd had a boy or a girl. My husband went with the medics. After about 30 minutes, a nurse confirmed that I had a daughter and she was fighting for her life. For two hours, no one could tell me whether she was going to live or die.

It was just two years since our first daughter had died. I couldn't countenance losing another little girl. If I am completely honest, I was too shattered and exhausted from the birth to stir my faith for her healing. In the midst of terrible distress, lying alone in a treatment room, I made a determined decision: "Whatever happens, I'm going to love God more, pray more and get more people saved."

Abigail was born on a Sunday morning. My husband texted every church leader he knew. Thousands of Christians prayed and our daughter pulled through against all the odds. What's more, despite being starved of oxygen, she suffered no lasting brain damage. She is now a top student and beautiful in every way. I am deeply grateful to the Lord for saving our daughter. I am thankful for one other thing too: the opportunity to show God that I love Him no matter what. Trying circumstances are some of our best opportunities to prove to the Lord that we love Him for who He is and not just for what He can do for us. We reach a point when we know for certain that we are in this for His glory and not for our comfort and ease.

Remember the three Hebrew men in Daniel's day who refused to worship the image created by King Nebuchadnezzar. They knew that God had the power to deliver them from the fiery furnace, yet they made a decision. Whether He saves me or not, I will serve Him anyway: "Our God whom we serve is able to deliver us from the burning fiery furnace, and He will deliver us from your hand, O king. But if not, let it be known to you, O king, that we do not serve your gods, nor will we worship the gold image which you have set up." Daniel 3:17-18

4. Compassion

Funnily enough, the fact that you have had to fight for every breakthrough is one indication that God has great things in store. When someone sails through life without any hindrances, they get an unrealistic view of the world. In order to reach us, God became like us and came to earth as a mere man. He endured pain and pressure so that He could relate to us: "We don't have a priest who is out of touch with our reality. He's been through weakness and testing, experienced it all - all but the sin." (Hebrews 4:15 - The Message)

After we suffer, we have a story that can help someone else to get free. When we suffer, it creates compassion for others when they face similar situations. As God restored me after the untimely death of our two-year-old daughter, I discovered that I had new expanses of love. The heartbreak plunged my soul to new depths. When God poured out His healing love, the result was new reservoirs of mercy. It was never the Lord's will for my little one to go so early but He turned the tragedy around for the benefit of many. My husband and I have had the privilege of ministering to countless couples across the world who have suffered the loss of a child. When they see our genuine happiness, they realize there is hope for them. Our tragedy has become a testimony which has led to the healing of many.

During times of trial, God pours out His love into our lives to such an extent that the drought becomes a pool deep enough to refresh others as well. It is the very comfort and strength that we receive in our trouble that God uses to minister to others. He does a work in us. Then out of the overflow, He can do a work through us: "He comes alongside us when we go through hard times, and before you know it, he brings us alongside someone else who is going through hard times so that we can be there for that person just as God was there for us." (2 Corinthians 1:4 - The Message). When we surrender our souls and our circumstances to the Lord, He can turn our mess into a message and our misery into a ministry. He will work all things together for our good and for the good of others.

129

As we are being transformed into strong pillars in God's kingdom, there are things we can do to help us come through. Here are a few...

The Word

Often as we endure, we ask Him to confirm that His word really is going to come to pass. We want Him to give us a fresh glimpse of the future. Sometimes, when we genuinely need the encouragement, He sends someone to reassure us. On other occasions, He knows that we have the faith and patience to possess His promise without any human intervention. God does not lie. He is always faithful. If He has said it, He will do it. We can choose to believe His Word whether we feel like it or not. That creates a testimony which is well worth sharing.

Abraham waited a long time for his promise to be fulfilled. He first heard God when he was 75 years of age. The Lord called him to leave home, promising to make him into a great nation. His second word was given after he suffered the pain of separation from his nephew Lot. The third was when Abraham reached rock bottom. Abraham received two more prophecies when he was 99 years old, one year before the promise was fulfilled. In twenty-five years, God gave Abraham five prophetic words. That's the equivalent of one every five years. There are occasions when we all need reassurance. However, our default position should always be to encourage ourselves with what God has *already* said. Go back to the promises you have been given. Get chapter and verse and believe His Word, despite your circumstances. Dig up and dust off those words that haven't yet materialized and get to work on them. That is faith and faith is what pleases God.

What are you focusing on?

I constantly remind myself to be thankful. In fact, I have a little picture on the wall beside my bed that says: 'Start each day with a grateful heart'. When I wake up, it reminds me to reset my heart. No matter what hasn't happened yet, there is always so much to be thankful for. My husband often jokes when he is preaching: "People ask me if I ever wake up grumpy. I tell them, 'No, she gets up at six!'" Fortunately, it is just a joke because I practice joy in the morning - even at six!

When I focus on my problems or on the disappointments of the past, it keeps me discouraged. When I look up and count my blessings, it puts today's trials into perspective: "For our present troubles are small and won't last very long. Yet they produce for us a glory that vastly outweighs them and will last forever! So we don't look at the troubles we can see now; rather, we fix our gaze on things that cannot be seen. For the things we see now will soon be gone, but the things we cannot see will last forever." (2 Corinthians 4:17-18 - New Living Translation)

A friend once said: "A bad attitude is like a flat tire. You can't move forward until you change it." What wisdom there is in those words. We have the power to choose our attitude. It takes self-control, but it is straightforward. As we take captive our thoughts, we can tell ourselves what to dwell on instead. Gratitude is a great attitude changer. Just stopping and thanking God for His goodness can transform the atmosphere. I might be fed up with my boss, but I can remind myself that I'm blessed to have a job. I could be struggling with my siblings, but I can instead thank God for my faithful friends. I have to take responsibility for my moods and change them when necessary.

Finding something to say thank you for should be easy for most of us. Let's do it, from the heart, right now. Stop reading for a moment to give God gratitude for every good gift He has *already* given you. The Lord loves a cheerful giver and thanksgiving is one of the best gifts we can give.

Praise is another key. It produces strength inside. It casts off the spirit of heaviness and shifts our focus from the problem to the Solver! We need to rejoice always and not just when all is well. It proves that we love God for who He is and not just for what He does. "In the day of prosperity be joyful, but in the day of adversity consider: Surely God has appointed the one as well as the other... " Ecclesiastes 7:14. Maintaining the right attitude when times are tough is one way of ushering in your new season. It also helps us prove our readiness for our promise.

Pass with flying colors!

God is always looking for an excuse to promote us. But He loves us too much to raise us up before we are ready. He watches how we respond to pain and pressure, looking for character and compassion. It helps me if I look at hard times as tests. It motivates me to do my best and to maintain the right attitude.

I remember discussing with my husband a dear leader in our church. This was someone who was sold out for God and really gifted. We were eager to promote them. However, they had character kinks that needed to be straightened out before we could contemplate giving them greater responsibility. That taught me a lesson. If we see the issues that are holding back our brothers and sisters, how much more does the Lord look on with longing for signs of growth in us? "But let these also first be tested; then let them serve as deacons having been found blameless." 1 Timothy 3:10

It takes several years for a student to get a degree. There are no substitutes for hard work. Typically, a university undergraduate faces challenging assessments and exams. Only after emerging successfully from this grueling process will they gain a degree. As a child of God, most of our training takes place at the university of adversity. Every fight is training your fingers for battle and your hands for war. Every battle won by faith is leading you closer to your victory.

Whatever you are facing, I encourage you to do what I do. Ask yourself: "Could this be a test?" Then rise to the challenge and determine that you will pass with flying colors. God is always looking for a reason to promote you. Every time you do well during adversity, He has a new excuse to bless you.

Prayer

Father God,

Thank You for the work that You are doing in me to make me a person You can really use. I ask You to strengthen me, to make me more resilient to the ups and downs of life. I ask You to build great character and maturity within so that others will see Your glory in me. I choose to see the difficulties I am facing right now as a test. I want to pass so I ask for Your help. I believe Your word to me and Your promises. I will endure and stay strong, even when I feel like giving up.

Thank You that You are making me into a pillar of strength!

In Jesus' name,

Amen

Declarations

The Word of God is powerful and it changes us. Take these Bible verses and speak them over your life:

> *"Blessed is the man who endures temptation; for when he has been approved, he will receive the crown of life which the Lord has promised to those who love Him." James 1:12*

> *"Consider it pure joy, my brothers and sisters, whenever you face trials of many kinds, because you know that the testing of your faith produces perseverance. Let perseverance finish its work so that you may be mature and complete, not lacking anything." James 1:2-4 (New International Version)*

> *"David encouraged and strengthened himself in the Lord his God." 1 Samuel 30:6*

Chapter 13

THE DREAM UNFOLDS

"Joseph's brothers came and bowed down before
him with their faces to the earth." Genesis 42:6b

After thirteen years of slavery and imprisonment, Joseph's day of
destiny finally arrived. In a matter of 24 hours, he went from
prison to palace and from felon to Pharaoh's number two. The God
who promised showed Himself faithful. Joseph was given a
position in government and quickly became the most important
leader of his time in that part of the world. One day he was a
convicted criminal and the next he was counsellor to the President.

God is not worried how your life will turn out. He is not looking
down from heaven wondering how to promote or prosper you. He
sees the end from the beginning. This means that He knows how
it is all going to work out. He is maneuvering you into position to
receive your blessing.

I think one of Joseph's greatest challenges probably came just
before his breakthrough. He interpreted the butler's dream and
believed this was his way out. But the King's employee forgot
about his friend in prison. Imagine if Joseph had given up on his
purpose. It would have been all too easy for him to think, "That's

the final straw. I must have been mad to believe this fairy tale. I'm throwing in the towel." Instead he stayed faithful and kept believing. And two years later, his day of destiny dawned.

Nearer than you know

I shall say it again. Your breakthrough is nearer now than it has ever been. When God gives us a vision, it is because *He* wants it to be fulfilled. Over and over again in Scripture it says, 'That it might be fulfilled'. God gives you a picture or a promise *that it might be fulfilled!* He does not give it to you to tantalize you. He gives it to you so that you can live to see it accomplished. If you are certain that it is God who gave you your dream, then don't let go. Don't give up. If you keep faith alive in your heart, the Lord will make sure you have a tremendous testimony to tell of His purposes being fulfilled.

When God places dreams in our hearts, they are *His* plans. He sows them inside us as motivating pictures and visions so that we will be inspired to do what it takes to attain them. Jeremiah 29:11 says, "For I know the plans I have for you, declares The Lord, plans to prosper you and not to harm you, plans to give you a hope and a future." These are God's purposes for your life. The process you have been going through is intended to prepare you for success. Your life, with all its twists and turns, is your training, your education and your finishing school all rolled into one. Keep your eye on your prize.

The dream

Nine years after Joseph's promotion, his dream played out before his eyes. Driven to Egypt by the terrible famine in Canaan, Joseph's brothers were brought before the governor responsible for distributing grain. They bowed themselves before their sibling. The eleven 'sheaves of corn' that he saw when he was just seventeen lay prostrate before him with their heads to the ground and begging for food.

I have often wondered why God gave Joseph dreams of himself rising high above his brothers. The Lord could have showed the teenager that he would one day be prime minister of a foreign country. Or He could have revealed that Joseph would be used to save two nations from famine. That would surely have been sufficiently inspiring and motivating. The advantage of such dreams is that they would probably be less open to misinterpretation. What do I mean? I know that I need to work hard in the pursuit of a humble heart. I believe that Joseph was no different. This vision featured the young man lording it over his brothers. It painted a picture of him in a position of superiority over his siblings.

The Lord gave him this promise at a time when he was favored by his father, treated better than his brothers and probably a bit arrogant! There was every chance it would make him proud. Then after he was betrayed and sold into slavery, the dream may have created a hunger for revenge! So I asked God about this and I believe He revealed a key. When Joseph no longer hankered after the humiliation of his siblings or his own superiority, God would have seen that he was prepared to become a servant leader. When the dream no longer impressed him, but instead stirred a longing for family reconciliation, God would have known, "My son is ready for his destiny."

Turning the tables

When storms are raging or tragedy hits, it can be overwhelming. Asking questions about our very purpose, we may query if God's hand is on our lives at all. I remember during the days and months after our daughter died, I wondered if I would ever recover. I couldn't understand why we had suffered this terrible loss or what we had done to deserve such sadness.

Truly, God causes all things to work together for good for those who love Him and are called according to His purpose. As I received my restoration, God gave me a new ministry of bringing comfort to others. I can honestly say that I do not regret the death of my firstborn. The depths of healing that God worked in me produced a quantity of compassion that I was not capable of carrying before. I have no pain or sadness remaining and yet God brought forth a river of compassion in me for others. It was shortly after our little one died that I told the Lord that I wanted to dedicate my life to bringing healing to the hurting. That dream has come to pass again and again the world over.

Joseph, who was once the victim, became the healer. After Jacob died, the brothers were worried that Joseph might withdraw his kindness. They sent word to him asking for forgiveness. Joseph was cut to the heart by their concerns and wept as he reassured them: "'Do not be afraid; I will provide for you and your little ones.' And he comforted them and spoke kindly to them." Genesis 50:21. Where Scripture says Joseph *spoke kindly* to his brothers, it literally means that he spoke to their hearts. You can only speak to someone's heart if God makes the way. Joseph's words penetrated any hard exterior and brought comfort and relief. The young ruler was not only used to save two nations from famine, but also to bring healing to his hurting family.

Your painful process

If you will let Him, God can give you a ministry out of your painful process. Because you were wounded, you can minister to others out of your healing. Whenever the Lord brings freedom to us, we can release to others what we have received: "God is our merciful Father and the source of all comfort. He comforts us in all our troubles so that we can comfort others. When they are troubled, we will be able to give them the same comfort God has given us." (2 Corinthians 1:3-4 - New Living Translation)

No matter how hard life has been, God can turn your circumstances around so that your tests become a heap of testimonies and your mess becomes a message that brings hope to many. I used to worry about the mistakes I had made until I realized that every time I fall, God can use my story of getting back up to reassure others that they too can rise up again after failure. As a result of that revelation, I have allowed my life to be an open book. There is no experience that the Lord can't use for His glory and the benefit of His kingdom.

One of the Lord's favorite pastimes is transformation. He specializes in turning our lives around. In the very areas where we have missed out or messed up, He brings restoration. "Instead of your shame you shall have double honor, and instead of confusion they shall rejoice in their portion. Therefore in their land they shall possess double; Everlasting joy shall be theirs." Isaiah 61:7.

A man of character

Joseph became one of the Bible's most honorable and loving leaders. He was transformed into a man of great character. As a result, he was able to handle the limelight without becoming self-important. He was able to lead a nation to salvation without believing he was God's greatest gift to mankind (even though he probably was at that time!). The process produced a person who could possess his promise. The period of preparation was painful. However, once he was ready, he was catapulted to prominence.

I have often thanked God that He never allowed me to rise higher than my character could carry me. For a long time it felt as though I was waiting in the wings while others took to the stage. Then I started to understand the kindness of God. He wants us to succeed in our mission. For that, our hearts need to be ready.

Saul was promoted to kingship in a matter of days. David endured more than a decade of delays before he was elevated. Saul did not handle promotion well. He even raised up monuments to himself. David, however, was prepared. He became not only Israel's most anointed king, but a source of inspiration to Christians across the world and throughout all generations. Jesus even calls Himself the son of David.

Hold on

Don't let the process of preparation dishearten you. You will reap in due season. Just don't lose heart. Hebrews says that 'By faith and patience' we lay hold of our promises. The One who gave us His Word is faithful to do it. Maintaining complete confidence that God can and will do it is your business. How it will happen is God's responsibility. The moment we start to worry about how, doubt and unbelief can creep into our hearts. We serve a very big God. He has a multitude of ways to do the impossible and bring every one of His plans for you to pass.

Joseph had no idea how he would ever get out of prison. That was not his problem. His job was to keep believing that God was able. Jacob did not know how he would face his furious brother Esau and come out alive. God did not ask him to figure that out. He told Jacob to believe and obey. Abraham had no clue how an impotent, elderly couple could possibly make a baby. But guess what? That was not his job. Abraham just had to believe that with the Lord all things are possible.

DOORWAY TO YOUR DESTINY

God always gives us some help along the way. Every time Sarah called out to her husband, he was reminded that he would become a father. Every time Abraham looked up or down, he was reminded that one day he would have descendants as numerous as the stars and the sand. Remind yourself continually of God's promises to you. Go back to the vision and return to your dream. Be faithful in what the Lord has asked of you and He will deliver right on time.

Suddenly

One of the many wonderful things about our God is that He loves surprises. That is why we see so many references to suddenly in Scripture. On the morning of his release from prison, Joseph probably woke up thinking it would be like any other day. Then the call came. Full of excitement, Joseph washed, shaved and changed out of his prison uniform into clothes fit for an interview with the king. He left prison ready for promotion.

No doubt the chatter around the palace will have gone something like this: "Where did this Hebrew come from? What a rapid rise to leadership!" They may say that about you when your day dawns. However, you and I know the truth. There is no such thing as an overnight success in God's kingdom. Very often we find that the longer the preparation, the greater the promotion. Keep your vision before your eyes. Your day of fulfilment is nearer now than it has ever been. When you do get your promise, by God's grace you'll be mature and resilient enough to keep hold of it too.

141

Prayer

Heavenly Father,

I want to thank You for Your awesome plans for my life. You have given me many precious promises and I know that You are always faithful to fulfil your purposes. My purpose is Your purpose so I know that it will come to pass.

I thank You that You promised so that You could fulfil. I thank You that You are more committed to my success than I am. I thank You that you see the end from the beginning and You know how my story unfolds. I trust You and I believe that You will do everything that You said You will do.

I will keep Your Word in front of my eyes. I will keep Your dream alive in my heart and I will keep believing, knowing that my breakthrough is closer than ever. I thank You for everything You have done and will do in me, through me and for me.

I give You all the glory.

In Jesus' name,

Amen.

Declarations

The Word of God is powerful and it changes us. Take these Bible verses and speak them over your life:

"I waited patiently and expectantly for the Lord; and He inclined to me and heard my cry." Psalms 40:1 (Amplified)

"Let us hold fast the confession of our hope without wavering, for He who promised is faithful." Hebrews 10:23

"Being confident of this very thing, that He who has begun a good work in you will complete it until the day of Jesus Christ." Philippians 1:6

"So shall My word be that goes forth from My mouth; it shall not return to Me void, but it shall accomplish what I please, and it shall prosper in the thing for which I sent it." Isaiah 55:11

Would you like to invite
Jesus into your heart?

If you would like to ask Jesus to become the Lord of your life, I would be honored to lead you in a simple prayer. The Bible says that God loves you and that Jesus wants to draw close:

> *"Behold I stand at the door and knock. If anyone hears My voice and opens the door, I will come in."*
> *Revelation 3:20*

If you would like to know Jesus as your friend, Lord and Savior, the first step is asking. Please pray this prayer:

Dear Lord,

I know that You love me and have a good plan for my life. I ask You to forgive me for all my sins. I invite You to come into my heart today and be my Lord. I give my life to You and ask You to lead me in Your ways from now on.

In Jesus' name,

Amen.

If you have prayed this prayer for the first time, it will be important to tell a Christian friend and find a good church. Just as a newborn baby needs nourishment and care, so you and I need the support of other believers as we start our new life as a follower of Jesus Christ.

You can listen free to Bible messages that will help to build your faith at www.harvestchurch.org.uk. You can also follow us on Facebook by searching for Harvest Church London or Jo Naughton.

About the Author

Jo Naughton is the founder of Healed for Life, a ministry dedicated to helping men and women be free to fulfil their God-given purpose. PR director turned pastor, Jo is an international speaker, author and a regular guest on TV and radio shows in the US and UK.

Jo ministers with a heart-piercing anointing, sharing with great personal honesty in conferences and at churches around the world. Her passion is to see people set free from all inner hindrances so that they can fulfil their God-given destiny. Countless people have testified to receiving powerful, life-changing emotional and spiritual healing through her ministry. Again and again, audiences share that they did not realize to what extent old issues or buried pain had been holding them back. The refreshment and freedom that so many people experience through Jo's ministry is transformational.

Together with her husband Paul, Jo pastors Harvest Church London in England and they have two wonderful children, Ben and Abby.

Healed for Life is a two day transformational event held in various nations throughout the year. Visit **www.jonaughton.com** for details. Jo has written three other life-changing books: 30 Day Detox for your Soul, Dreamstealers and Lifting the Mask. Her husband, Paul has written: Welcome to Ziklag.

Visit **www.jonaughton.com** for details about Healed for life, her books, her weekly blog and for updates of where she is ministering.

Also by this author:

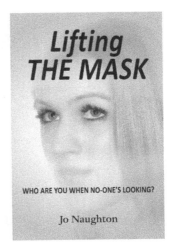

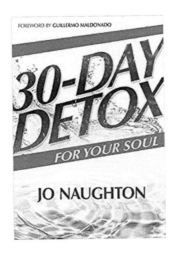

All Jo Naughton's books are available at: <u>jonaughton.com</u>

Ingram Content Group UK Ltd.
Milton Keynes UK
UKHW020046210623
423745UK00014B/402